Endorsements

God's Word will leap off the pages and into your heart as you read through the message Wendy shares in *Living So That*. I love how she guides readers through practical application and deep Bible study, while teaching us the "so that" truths that God gives us in His Word. It's simple, yet challenging, and I can't wait to lead an online Bible study of this book! This is truth we all need in our lives!

—Melissa Taylor
  Director of Online Bible Studies, Proverbs 31 Ministries

Living So That will woo you to engage in deep personal study of the word of God in fresh ways. Wendy Blights in depth research is stimulating, her vulnerable self-reflection is authentic and her abiding relationship with Christ will embolden you to go deeper, stay longer and be transformed!

—Tracey Eyster
  Founder/Executive Director of FamilyLife's MomLifeToday.com
  & author of *Be The Mom*

living so that

MAKING FAITH-FILLED CHOICES in the MIDST of a MESSY LIFE

WENDY BLIGHT

THOMAS NELSON
Since 1798

NASHVILLE DALLAS MEXICO CITY RIO DE JANEIRO

Published in Nashville, Tennessee, by Thomas Nelson. Thomas Nelson is a registered trademark of HarperCollins Christian Publishing, Inc.

Author represented by Erik S. Wolgemuth; Wolgemuth and Associates, Inc.

Page design and layout: Crosslin Creative

Thomas Nelson, Inc., titles may be purchased in bulk for educational, business, fund-raising, or sales promotional use. For information, please e-mail SpecialMarkets@ThomasNelson.com.

Unless otherwise noted, Scripture quotations are taken from *The Voice*™ translation. © 2012 Ecclesia Bible Society. Used by permission. All rights reserved.

Scripture quotations designated "Amplified Bible" are taken from The Amplified Bible: Old Testament. ©1962, 1964 by Zondervan (used by permission); and from THE AMPLIFIED BIBLE: NEW TESTAMENT. © 1958 by the Lockman Foundation (used by permission).

Scripture quotations marked ESV are taken from The English Standard Version. © 2001 by Crossway Bibles, a division of Good News Publishers.

Scripture quotations designated as being from the J. B. Phillips version are taken from J. B. Phillips: THE NEW TESTAMENT IN MODERN ENGLISH, Revised Edition. © J. B. Phillips 1958, 1960, 1972. Used by permission of Macmillan Publishing Co., Inc.

Scriptures marked KJV are from the King James Version (public domain).

Scripture quotations marked NIV are taken from the Holy Bible, New International Version® NIV®. Copyright © 1973, 1978, 1984, 2011 by Biblica, Inc.™ Used by permission of Zondervan. All rights reserved worldwide. www.zondervan.com

Scripture quotations marked NKJV are taken from THE NEW KING JAMES VERSION. © 1982 by Thomas Nelson, Inc. Used by permission. All rights reserved.

Scripture quotations marked NLT are taken from the *Holy Bible*, New Living Translation. © 1996, 2004, 2007. Used by permission of Tyndale House Publishers, Inc., Carol Stream, Illinois 60188. All rights reserved.

ISBN: 9781401679255

Printed in the United States of America

14 15 16 17 18 RRD 6 5 4 3 2 1

Dedication

To Jan Harrison, my first Bible teacher and the first person who modeled what it means to truly have a passionate love for God's Word. How incredibly thankful I am for the blessing to have sat at your feet and learned from you. Your love for Jesus and His Word is fiercely contagious, and I'm only one of many who have caught the fever! Thank you for the love, time, and prayer you have invested in me and, in turn, my family and my ministry. I love you and am forever grateful.

Acknowledgments

Many people contributed to the creation and completion of this study. I treasure and am so thankful for each one.

To Monty, you are the love of my life and my very best friend; thank you for being my biggest cheerleader.

To Lauren and Bo, being your mom is my highest calling and brings me my greatest joy.

To John and Connie Rotty, my parents, thank you for your love and encouragement.

To David Chadwick, my pastor and friend, your preaching series planted the truths in my heart that launched this study.

To Living Truth Bible Study in Charlotte, North Carolina, with you I have experienced the richness of what it means to truly belong to the body of Christ.

To Lysa TerKeurst, you model "so that" living and have shown me what it means to live sacrificially for God's glory.

To my Proverbs 31 sisters, thank you for pouring into my life; I love doing ministry with you.

To Ashley, Frank, Maleah, Alee, and the production team at Thomas Nelson Publishers, thank you for allowing me to partner with you as a Bible teacher; you are not just names and faces with whom I work; you are dear friends and partners in ministry.

To Lisa Sheltra, my dear friend, traveling companion, and editor; I could not do what I do without you.

To Karen Cauthen, my heart sister, thank you for praying for me and always believing in me; you are a treasured gift from Jesus.

To Erik, Robert, and Bobbie Wolgemuth, thank you for investing in my life and ministry; I am so thankful for each one of you.

To my prayer warriors, thank you for interceding on my behalf and on behalf of those whose lives will be changed through this study.

Contents

Introduction

Welcome to *Living So That: Making Faith-Filled Choices in the Midst of a Messy Life*. I am excited you have chosen to take this journey with me! As I wrote each page, I prayed for every woman God would lead to join in our adventure. Begin confident, sweet friend, that you will meet God in the pages of His Word and this book. He promises us in Isaiah 55:11 that when His Word goes out, it will not return empty. God will reveal Himself with every turn of the page. You will learn new truths about God, His character, His purposes for you, and most especially, His incredible love for you.

You can do *Living So That* individually or with a small group. I encourage a small group setting because it allows for accountability and rich discussions with other women about what you have learned.

You will notice that several different translations are used in this study, mainly The Voice and the New International Version (1984). If you don't own either of these translations, you will still be able to work through the lessons. In fact, using several versions while you study God's Word will only enhance your understanding. *Living So That* takes you through five chapters of "so that" scriptures in the New Testament. Each chapter begins with a Memory Verse and a Prayer. I encourage you to pray the prayer as you open your Bible to study. Remember, the Holy Spirit is your teacher, so praying prepares your heart to receive all that God has for you. And please don't let the memory verses intimidate you. I give you lots of encouragement in chapter 1 about memorizing scripture.

Each chapter is divided into five sections, and each section includes Application Questions, If You Want to Go Deeper Questions (most sections), and Concluding Thought Questions. We leave space for you to write your answers, but I encourage you to get a journal or notebook to write in as well. Set aside special time each day to complete your reading and study. Ask the Lord to help you make it a priority.

living so that ←←←

At the close of each chapter, I invite you to participate in a Call to Action as a way to help you apply practically what you are learning. When answering the Call to Action, think about the ways God has spoken to you and what He wants you to do in response. We are not studying God's Word to increase our head knowledge. We are studying His Word so that God can change our hearts and our lives! John 15:5 promises that our lives will yield beautiful fruit if we will abide in Christ. One way to do that is by studying His Word. So surrender your heart and your time to Him, turn the page, and let's begin!

CHAPTER ONE

Jesus Came So That...

MEMORY VERSE: FOR GOD SO LOVED THE WORLD THAT HE GAVE HIS ONE AND ONLY SON, **[SO] THAT** WHOEVER BELIEVES IN HIM SHALL NOT PERISH BUT HAVE ETERNAL LIFE.

—John 3:16 (NIV; emphasis added)

MESSAGE FROM MY HEART

God's Word is my most cherished possession, and each book I write emerges from the fruit of God's work in and through my time with Him in His Word. My deepest desire as you journey through this book is for you to gain great confidence in your ability to read, understand, and practically apply God's Word.

Every time I open my Bible to write a new book, I invite God to do a "new thing." He is always faithful, and this book is no different. As God birthed *Living So That,*

He worked each and every lesson in my own heart before I crafted a single page.

Be encouraged as we begin, my friend. Whether it is your first time studying the Bible or your tenth, God will be at work in our midst. Why? Because His Word is living and active, sent to transform us from the inside out. The Bible is not just a history book. It's not just a biography. It's not a "how to" book. It is a living book from our Father in heaven, filled with truths and promises intended to speak not only to its original audience but to us today.

But for His Word to work from the inside out in our lives, we must first take it into our hearts. Listen to the words of the prophet Jeremiah:

> When I discovered Your words, I ate them up: they were my great joy and my heart's delight. *I am Yours, and* I bear the name of the Eternal God. (Jeremiah 15:16)

Allowing God's Word to work in us requires digesting His Word. But digestion can only occur by first ingesting God's Word. Yes, we must read God's Word. But more than that, we must study it and allow it to permeate our hearts and minds. Sometimes it's hard to discipline ourselves to do this. We struggle to remember items on our grocery lists, friends' cell phone numbers, and activities on our "to do" lists, so we think, *How could I ever memorize God's Word?* To help us in this endeavor, I included a memory verse in each chapter. My prayer is that you will make every effort to prayerfully commit these verses to memory and hide them in your heart.

When I began writing this book, I invited my family to participate in the scripture memory portions. They moaned and groaned. Their excuse: "I can't memorize scripture." I quickly pointed out how they

Allowing God's Word to work in us requires digesting His Word.

constantly belt out lyrics to their favorite songs, entertain me with lines from their favorite movies, and recite hilarious skits from their favorite YouTube videos.

Really, these are things we all do. I share with you what I shared with my family: If we can so easily remember catchy lyrics and memorable movie lines, how much more should we seek to remember the precious words of our Lord and Savior?

So, as a family, we committed to memory the verses in this book. Each week I wrote the verse on a plate in our kitchen. We divided the verse into sections to make it easier to memorize and repeated each section to one another, adding a new part each day. At the end of the week, we recited the full verse and celebrated together the promise we now had hidden in our hearts. (Okay, my fifteen-year-old son did not necessarily celebrate, but I did!)

If we can so easily remember catchy lyrics and memorable movie lines, how much more should we seek to remember the precious words of our Lord and Savior?

Will you join us in doing the same? If you don't have a plate like ours, post the verse in places around your house where you spend the most time. Then, using the same tactic we did, memorize a few sections at a time. We have friends who painted a door in their kitchen with chalk paint and posted their weekly verses on the door. Another friend bought an index card notebook for each family member. They wrote each week's verse in their binders and kept them in the kitchen. Find the way that works best for you. Invite a friend, family member, roommate, spouse, or another Bible study member to join you. This is not a requirement, my friend. But if you decide to say yes, I promise that God will richly bless you as you hide His Word in your heart.

⋙ PRAYER:

Father, today begins a new day in my spiritual journey with You. Thank You for bringing me to this book . . . for setting apart this time and place for me to be in Your Word. As I begin my first chapter, I come boldly before Your throne, asking to be filled with the full, deep, and clear knowledge of Your will for me in this season of my life. Please use my time here to invigorate, refresh, strengthen, and renew me. Father, speak truth into my life . . . even hard truth. Your Word calls me to action. You call me to a life that will make a difference for You and Your kingdom. Open my eyes to see that life. Give me a heart that desires that life above all else.

If I am not living in a way that pleases You or loving others in a way that honors You or studying Your Word in a way that changes me, convict my heart by speaking truth in love. Make my heart tender to receive Your rebuke and discipline. You have drawn me here, and I want to receive ALL You have for me!

Father, bring Your living and active Word alive in my heart. Invade every part of my being. Transform me from the inside out! Amen.

PART ONE:
Introduction

As I sought direction for my next Bible study, God began to impress two words on my heart: "so that." Sounds strange, doesn't it? I thought so, too, because in response to past prayers for direction on study topics, God had always led me to a book of the Bible. It was clear. But not this time. This time it was just two simple words. "So that." I hesitated. *Lord, how can I write an entire book based on only two words?*

The words were not random. A few years ago, my church began a campaign to raise money to plant two new churches. The project's name was "So That." The goal, and the message that accompanied it, was not only to raise funds, but to challenge our church body to live a "so that" life rather than a "so what?" life. Meaning: our lives should not be self-centered and static; rather, they should be others-centered and active, making a difference for the kingdom of God.

At the time, I listened to the sermons, faithfully wore my "So That" bracelet, and gave financially. When the campaign was over, those two little words never left me. The question lingered. What does it really mean to live a "so that" life? Was it simply a catchy campaign slogan, or was it something to which God truly calls us?

The question led me to research, as it often does. My educational background is in law, and I worked as a lawyer for about four

> Our lives should not be self-centered and static; rather, they should be others-centered and active, making a difference for the kingdom of God.

years, so researching comes naturally to me. I dug into God's Word, searching for as many "so that" verses as I could find. It became a monumental task, so I quickly limited my research to the New Testament. And it was there that God began a most amazing and life-changing journey.

"So that" verses came alive to me as never before. In fact, the number of verses I found in the book of John alone blew me away! Though I had read this gospel through many times, and had even taught it, never before had I noticed these particular verses. When I began *intentionally* searching, they appeared everywhere. What I found was that Hebrews 4:12 is absolutely true: God's Word is "living and active" (NIV)! Friend, this is what is so powerful about the Word of God. No matter how often we read it, we receive something fresh and new each time.

No matter how often we read the Word of God, we receive something fresh and new each time.

I delved deeper, extending my research beyond Scripture. Several theologians had pursued this same path. In Greek grammar, a "so that" statement is known as a *hina* clause. It is a purpose clause used in conjunction with a subjunctive participle. Before you close your book and sprint in the other direction, please indulge my inner geek. There is an important point here.

A subjunctive participle sets the mood of a sentence. It generally indicates possibility or probability that something might happen. Often-used subjunctive participles in Scripture are "may" and "might." A modern example of this would be, "I *might* eat dinner with you, if I feel like it." Whether I eat dinner with you depends on how I feel, so I may or may not eat with you.

But when an author uses a *hina* clause ("so that") in conjunction with a subjunctive participle, it changes the mood of the sentence from one of possibility or probability to one of purpose or result.

Consequently, if I change the sentence above to read, "I brought dinner *so that* we might eat together," the second statement contains a purpose. I brought dinner, so you know with certainty that we will have dinner together. It's a promise.

The authors of Scripture knew this distinction and, led by the Spirit, intentionally chose to use these two words to connect a truth of Scripture to a practical application of that truth. They used them to bring truth alive and make it relevant and applicable to our everyday lives.

Life is messy, and God knows that. One of the reasons He gave us the Bible is to equip us to live out our faith in the midst of our messy lives. Each new day can bring with it a myriad of issues and problems. And each one requires us to make a choice. We can choose to make "faith-*filled*" choices, or we can choose to make "faith-*less*" choices. The faith-*less* choices tend to come easier for most of us. They occur when we react quickly out of our emotions and basically "do what comes naturally." And more often than not, those choices have negative consequences that hurt not only us but also everyone with whom we come in contact.

Faith-filled choices are harder to make. They occur when we react not out of our emotions but out of a Spirit-led heart and mind. And faith-filled choices have good consequences that bless not only us but also those around us.

Each day we make choices. Through the next several chapters, we will study a multitude of "so that" verses that will provide guidance on how to make those choices. The Scriptures and many personal stories will equip us with tools *so that* by the end of this book, we will know how to make more faith-filled choices and fewer faith-less choices.

Because these verses cover a wide variety of topics, too many to cover in one book, we will focus on the following themes:

1. Jesus came so that . . .

2. God spoke so that . . .

3. Pray so that . . .

4. Trials come so that . . .

5. Let your light shine so that . . .

When we see phrases such as "so that" repeated in Scripture, it's significant. In fact, anything our Father in heaven sees fit to repeat hundreds of times throughout His Word is something to which we should pay great attention.

Proverbs 4:1 says, "*Gather,* children, to hear your father's instruction. Pay close attention so you will understand."

Anticipate all that God wants to teach you through your time in this book! Pay attention to what you read. Invite God to give you a fresh understanding of His timeless Word . . . especially those verses and passages you may already know and love. Pray and prepare your heart to receive the "new thing" He wants to do in your heart!

In the next section we will begin with our first "so that": "Jesus came so that . . ." Before you turn the page,

Share *your* thoughts as to why Jesus came to earth.

PART TWO:

The Law

MEMORY VERSE: FOR GOD SO LOVED THE WORLD THAT HE GAVE HIS ONE AND ONLY SON, **[SO] THAT** WHOEVER BELIEVES IN HIM SHALL NOT PERISH BUT HAVE ETERNAL LIFE.

—John 3:16 (NIV; emphasis added)

Why did Jesus so willingly leave the splendor of heaven to enter the squalor of earth? Our journey begins by answering this very question as we examine God's plan behind sending Jesus to earth.

Read Romans 5:20–21:

> When the law came into the picture, sin grew and grew; but wherever sin grew and spread, God's grace was there in fuller, greater measure. *No matter how much sin crept in, there was always more grace.* In the same way that sin reigned in the sphere of death, now grace reigns through God's restorative justice, *eclipsing death and* leading to eternal life through the Anointed One, Jesus our Lord, *the Liberating King.*

In Scripture, when we see the words "the law," they refer to God's law for His people.

The best-known laws of God are the _____

_____ . (Hint: Exodus 34:28 NIV)

God used His commandments (the law) as an instrument to teach His people in very specific ways about sin. The law *pointed out* people's sin, thereby making them aware of it. Romans 7:7 says:

> So what is the story? Is the law itself sin? Absolutely not! *It is the exact opposite.* I would never have known what sin is if it were not for the law. *For example*, I would not have known that desiring

something that belongs to my neighbor is sin if the law had not said, "You are not to covet."

The law reveals the presence and fact of sin, but what happens next is frightening. Paul wrote, "Sin took advantage of the commandment to create a constant stream of greed and desire within me; *I began to want everything.* You see, apart from the law, sin lies dormant" (Romans 7:8).

Paul tells us in Romans 7:8 that sin takes advantage of or "seiz[es] the opportunity" (NIV) found in the law. The word for opportunity here is *aphorme*. This word denotes a starting point, often referred to as a base of operations in war. By choosing this word, God was warning us that the law provides sin with a base of operations for its attack upon the soul. Dr. David Jeremiah says that sin uses the commandment, or the law, as a beachhead from which to launch its evil work.[1] Consequently, because of our sinful nature, when something is forbidden, the law makes us aware of it and we desire to do it all the more.

Let me make this a bit more real. I experienced this firsthand as a young mother. When my daughter was little, every time she accompanied me on a shopping trip, I sternly warned, "Lauren, do not touch. You may look with your eyes, but do not touch." Sound familiar? I repeated this phrase many times.

On one particular trip, I knew the temptation to touch would be overwhelming. We were going to the Christmas store, packed with hundreds of shelves filled with glittery ornaments and glistening decorations that little girls cannot resist. Thus, I gave extra warnings.

We oohed and aahed over all the baubles. Then, after I chose and paid for my gifts, Lauren and I headed to the car.

As I lifted her out of her stroller, something shiny caught my eye. It was an ornament . . . one I had neither chosen nor paid for. My sweet little girl had stolen it. A thief at age three! I informed her we had to return the ornament and that she would have to apologize. Tears flooded her eyes and spilled down her cheeks. She begged, "You say it, Mommy . . . *pweeese*." I stood my ground, explaining that when we break a rule and take what is not ours, there are consequences. We walked back into the store and found the clerk, and Lauren, with head bowed and shoulders slumped, handed her loot to the clerk and whispered, "I'm sorry."

My instructions forbidding her to touch the beautiful items in the store made her want to touch them all the more. That is how it is with the law, Paul said. In order to understand the goodness of the law, we need a maturity that often takes time to develop. God didn't give us the law to set us up for failure; rather, He gave us the law to protect us from failure. God's standards would exist whether or not we ever knew about them. But in His mercy God informed us of His law and has shown us the only way to fulfill it—through faith in Jesus Christ.

Now, let's dig a bit deeper into the passage in Romans. Romans 8:1–2 says:

> Therefore, now no condemnation awaits those who are living in Jesus the Anointed, *the Liberating King,* because when you live in the Anointed One, Jesus, *a new law takes effect.* The law of the Spirit of life *breathes into you and* liberates you from the law of sin and death.

In this verse, we find two governing principles that work within the law of God.

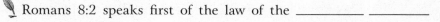 Romans 8:2 speaks first of the law of the _____ _____ _____ .

The law of the Spirit of life operates through God's Holy Spirit (our new nature). His spirit is a life-giving Spirit.

living so that ⟵⟵

Romans 8:2 also speaks of the law of _____ _____

_____ .

The law of sin and death operates through the flesh (our sin nature). It ultimately produces death.

Sin operates in our flesh and causes us to succumb to temptation and disobey the commands of God. The Holy Spirit, who is stronger and mightier than the flesh, enables us to fully overcome that temptation and obey the commands of God. Said another way, the Spirit of life frees us from being held captive by the law of sin and death.

⟫ APPLICATION:

As always, God's Word speaks consistent truths throughout its pages.

Read Galatians 3:10–14, 23–25. What happens to those who refuse God's offer of grace and insist on being made right with God through obeying the law? (v. 10)

According to this passage, how can we be made right with God (be made righteous)? (v. 11)

How have we been redeemed? (v. 13; see also Deuteronomy 21:22–23)

Jesus died on the cross *so that* what? (v. 14)

Summarize the truths in Galatians 3:23–25 in your own words. What does this mean for your life?

IF YOU WANT TO GO DEEPER:

Read the verses that follow and take notes on what each verse speaks to you about

1. the purpose of the law

2. how it relates to sin

3. Jesus' role as it relates to the law and sin

Don't be concerned about getting the "right" answer. Just invite the Holy Spirit to open your heart to receive and understand the spiritual truths in these verses. Write what you hear.

• Moreover the law entered *[so] that* the offense might abound. But where sin abounded, grace abounded much more, *so that* as sin reigned in death, even so grace might reign through righteousness to eternal life through Jesus Christ our Lord. (Romans 5:20–21 NKJV; emphasis added)

• So, my brothers, you also died to the law through the body of Christ, [*so*] *that* you might belong to another, to him who was raised from the dead, *in order that* we might bear fruit to God. For when we were controlled by the sinful nature, the sinful passions aroused by the law were at work in our bodies, *so that* we bore fruit for death. But now, by dying to what once bound us, we have been released from the law *so that* we serve in the new way of the Spirit, and not in the old way of the written code. (Romans 7:4–6 NIV; emphasis added)

• Did that which is good, then, become death to me? By no means! But *in order that* sin might be recognized as sin, it produced death in me through what was good, *so that* through the commandment sin might become utterly sinful. (Romans 7:13 NIV; emphasis added)

• Before this faith came, we were held prisoners by the law, locked up until faith should be revealed. So the law was put in charge to lead us to Christ [*so*] *that* we might be justified by faith. (Galatians 3:23–24 NIV; emphasis added)

CONCLUDING THOUGHTS:

The bottom line here is grace, my friend. Grace came first, and the law came alongside grace. This had been a part of God's plan since the beginning of time. Grace began in the garden of Eden, when God covered Adam and Eve with animal skins. Grace continued as God extended it to the hard-hearted Israelites throughout the Old Testament. Jesus lived and extended grace throughout His entire ministry. Even after Jesus' death, grace continued as He, through His disciples, extended grace beyond the Jews to the Gentiles. And now He extends grace to you and me.

Grace is undeserved. It makes no sense in the world's economy. In one of His last acts, Jesus forgave the thief hanging on the cross beside Him and told him he would be with Him that day in paradise. It didn't matter to Jesus what motivated this man's confession. Jesus still forgave him. He forgave him knowing he would never study the Bible, never impact the kingdom, and never bring another to Christ. What a wonderful, beautiful reminder that you and I do not have to *do anything* to earn God's grace. It's a free gift. Grace does not depend on what we have done, but on what God has done for us.

Because of God's grace, we are no longer bound by the law of sin and death. Praise God! We are free because of His amazing grace.

Spend a few minutes meditating on the words of John Newton's famous hymn, "Amazing Grace."

> Amazing Grace, how sweet the sound,
> That saved a wretch like me.
> I once was lost but now am found,
> Was blind, but now I see.
>
> T'was Grace that taught my heart to fear.
> And Grace, my fears relieved.
> How precious did that Grace appear
> The hour I first believed.

Through many dangers, toils and snares
I have already come;
'Tis Grace that brought me safe thus far
And Grace will lead me home.

The Lord has promised good to me.
His word my hope secures.
He will my shield and portion be,
As long as life endures.

Yea, when this flesh and heart shall fail,
And mortal life shall cease,
I shall possess within the veil
A life of joy and peace.

When we've been there ten thousand years
Bright shining as the sun,
We've no less days to sing God's praise
Than when we've first begun.

Friend, you have spent significant time in God's Word. You have studied, pondered, and prayed over our first "so that." Based on how God has spoken to your heart, complete the thought below.

Jesus came so that . . .

PART THREE:
New Life

MEMORY VERSE: FOR GOD SO LOVED THE WORLD THAT HE
GAVE HIS ONE AND ONLY SON, **[SO] THAT** WHOEVER BELIEVES IN
HIM SHALL NOT PERISH BUT HAVE ETERNAL LIFE.

—John 3:16 (NIV; emphasis added)

Now that grace has set us free from the law of sin and death, what
comes next?

Read Romans 6:4:

> Therefore, we were buried with Him through this baptism into
> death **so that** just as God the Father, in all His glory, resurrected
> the Anointed One, we, too, might walk *confidently out of the grave
> into a new life.* (Bold emphasis added)

According to this verse, God extended grace *so that* what?

What comes next is spiritual baptism. The very moment you
and I confess our sin and accept Jesus Christ as our Lord and Savior,
we become one with Christ. We are in Him, and He in us. Do you
know what this means, my friend? It means the Spirit of the living God deposits Himself in us! The God who created the heavens
and the earth . . . who counts the stars and calls them by name . . .
who provides rain for the earth and causes the grass to grow . . . who
sends snow like white wool and hurls down hail like stones . . .
who heals the lame and makes the blind to see . . . *chooses* to live

inside you and me. Before we move on, will you join me in thanking God for this most precious gift?

Heavenly Father, thank You for the gift of grace. Thank You that in the midst of my sin, You made a way to enter into my heart to cleanse me from all unrighteousness. Thank You for removing my sin as far as the east is from the west. Thank You for entering into this wretched heart of mine to cleanse it and make me a new creation. Thank You for choosing to place Your Holy Spirit inside of me to mold me and shape me from the inside out and make me more like You. I love You and am forever grateful for this new life You have given me. I pray this in Jesus' name. Amen.

Dr. Kenneth Wuest, a New Testament Greek scholar and Bible translator, in his book *Romans in the Greek New Testament*, defines the word "baptize," as used in this verse, as the "introduction or placing of a person or thing into a new environment or into union with something else so as to alter its condition or its relationship to its previous environment or condition."[2] I just love this description. God places His Spirit in us to unite with us and change us forever!

In other words, upon baptism, a new thing happens within us that changes the old.

APPLICATION:

This brings us to the next phase of God's plan for the life of His Son. This plan required not only Jesus' physical death but also His burial. Both were necessary to prove Christ actually died. But death was not the end for Jesus. On the third day, Scripture teaches, He rose from the grave in a newly resurrected body with a new mission.

Why is this significant for us?

At the moment of our salvation, we, too, like Christ, die and are buried. But ours is a spiritual rather than a physical death. Our sin nature, our "old self," dies with Christ. And just as Jesus was raised from the dead into new life, we, too, are raised from spiritual death to a new spiritual life. The phrase "new life" comes from the word "newness," which in the Greek means "life of a new quality." We have a new spirit living within us. This new life is different. It's not as though we died and someone resuscitated us. It is a totally fresh, new beginning! The old has gone and the new has come.

A few years ago, this truth came alive for me as I watched my son's baptism. When the weather cooperates, our church baptizes outside in pools. After our morning service, we headed out to the church lawn, where family and friends circled the pool. Bo climbed up the stairs to the deck a bit nervous, not sure what to expect. Each step he took caused my heart to skip a beat. This was, after all, answered prayer for this mom. Soon he began to lower himself into the pool and when he reached the bottom step, Bo walked toward Nick, his life group leader. Nick reminded him of all he had learned in the "Next Steps" class he had just finished. He then asked Bo if he was ready to take this next step in his faith. Bo said yes and answered each of Nick's questions. As he answered the last one, Nick dunked Bo under the water and raised him back up. A smile like I have never seen lit up Bo's face. He climbed out of the pool to be showered with hugs all around.

Bo being raised up out of that water created a beautiful picture in my mind of the new life we have in Christ. Baptism, in whatever form, is God's way of enabling us to identify with and experience Christ's death, burial, and resurrection.

Baptism says to the whole world, "I belong to Christ!" Never again do we have to feel as though we don't belong or we don't fit in. Our identity is in Christ and Christ alone. Read the words of Peter:

> Blessed is God, the Father of our Lord Jesus, the Anointed One! Because He has raised Jesus the Anointed from death, through His great mercy we have been reborn into a living hope—reborn for an eternal inheritance, held in reserve in heaven, that will never fade or fail. (1 Peter 1:3–4)

We may not understand everything about baptism or agree on how it should be done, but what we can agree on is that salvation and baptism together change us from the inside out. We are no longer lost, alone and without hope. We each have a new identity as God's adopted child, redeemed by the blood of Jesus, sealed with the Holy Spirit. And no matter what happens in this life, my friend, nothing will ever change that!

Read **Galatians 2:19–20** and share how this verse relates to our discussion.

Read **John 11:1–44.** Reread verses 43 and 44. Share how Lazarus's story relates to our conversation.

Let's take a look at Lazarus's story and how it ties in to our discussion. Lazarus was a friend of Jesus who died while Jesus was in another town. When Jesus arrived in Bethany, Lazarus had been in the grave four days. There was no doubt that he was dead. Upon reaching the cave where Lazarus was buried, Jesus prayed. After He prayed, He cried three words: "Lazarus, come out!" (John 11:43). Pay attention here. Simply by His spoken word, Jesus raised Lazarus from the dead.

Immediately Lazarus came out. When he appeared, grave clothes bound his hands and feet. Jesus spoke again: "Take off the grave clothes and let him go" (John 11:44 NIV). The New King James Version says, "Loose him, and let him go."

This powerful story gives us another visual for the spiritual truths we are learning. When Jesus gives us new life, He strips away all that binds us . . . all that holds us captive . . . and frees us so we can be fully alive to enter into a new life with Him.

Do you live in this freedom, or do you live bound up in grave clothes, held captive by bitterness, unforgiveness, anger, fear, doubt, sickness, or something else? Friend, Jesus wants you to live and walk in the freedom of the cross.

Read Romans 6:6–7:

> For we know that our old self was crucified with him *so that* the body of sin might be done away with, that we should no longer be slaves to sin—because anyone who has died has been freed from sin. (NIV; emphasis added)

The term "old self" (the New King James Version uses the words "old man") refers to the spiritual person each of us was before we came to know and love Jesus as our Lord and Savior. It is the person we each used to be *in Adam* (Romans 5:12).

"Body of sin" does not refer to the sin that resides in us. It refers more to the fact that our bodies are used as instruments of sin. Before Christ, our physical bodies were ruled and controlled by sin. We were slaves to sin.

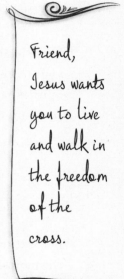

Friend, Jesus wants you to live and walk in the freedom of the cross.

But Jesus came and freed us from that sin. We are no longer slaves to the law of sin and death. Praise Jesus, because of the gift of grace, we are *free*!

The effect of this transaction is powerful. Paul wrote that upon salvation, the body of sin was "done away with" (NIV); other translations say "destroyed." What exactly does this mean? He was not saying salvation eradicated the body of sin. It did not. We still live in our same bodies. Rather, it nullified it. The Greek word *katargeo* here means "to reduce to inactivity." Salvation renders sin powerless and ineffective.

If sin no longer controls those who are believers in Jesus, who or what controls them?

Share a time in your life when you felt the struggle/battle between your flesh, the sin nature that still resides within you, and the Holy Spirit, the new nature that now controls you? How did your situation turn out? What did you learn through the process?

An important point is made here. Yes, we have been made free, but we must *choose* every day to live in that freedom. We still live in the mortal bodies into which we were born. Sin is still present in us because of our sin nature, and it fights to be top dog in our hearts and minds.

Our flesh is weak. The Holy Spirit is strong. We can feed one nature or the other. The one we feed most will be the one to gain power. Feed the flesh, and it will prevail. Feed the Spirit, and it will prevail. Our actions impact the outcome of this battle. The choices we make every day determine the victor.

Romans 6:12–14 says, "Therefore do not let sin reign in your mortal body *so that* you obey its evil desires. Do not offer the parts of your body to sin, as instruments of wickedness, but rather offer yourselves to God, as those who have been brought from death to life; and offer the parts of your body to him as instruments of righteousness. For sin shall not be your master, because you are not under law, but under grace" (NIV; emphasis added).

This same passage in the J. B. Phillips translation says, "Do not, then, allow sin to establish any power over your mortal bodies in making you give way to your lusts. Nor hand over your organs to be, as it were, weapons of evil for the devil's purposes. But, like men rescued from certain death, put yourselves in God's hands as weapons of good for his own purposes. For sin is not meant to be your master—you are no longer living under the Law, but under grace."

The Voice translation reads:

> Don't invite *that insufferable tyrant of* sin back into your mortal body **so [that]** you won't become obedient to its *destructive* desires. Don't offer your bodily members to sin's service as tools of wickedness; instead, offer your body to God as those who are alive from the dead, and devote the parts of your body to God as tools for justice *and goodness in this world*. For sin is no longer a tyrant over you; indeed you are under grace and not the law. (Bold emphasis added)

Never forget these two natures are diametrically opposed to one another and one will prevail. Galatians 5:16–17 says it well:

> So I say, walk by the Spirit, and you will not gratify the desires of the flesh. For the flesh desires what is contrary to the Spirit, and the Spirit what is contrary to the flesh. They are in conflict with each other, *so that* you do not do what you want. (NIV; emphasis added)

🖋 Contrast ways to feed the flesh and ways to feed the spirit. (See Romans 12:9–21.)

🖋 How do you feed your spirit?

🖋 If you feel your flesh is winning in this struggle, commit today to take one step toward feeding your spirit and write a prayer of commitment below.

→》CONCLUDING THOUGHTS:

🖋 Friend, you have spent significant time in God's Word. You have studied, pondered, and prayed over the "new life" we have in Christ. Based on how God has spoken to your heart, complete the thought below.

Jesus came so that . . .

PART FOUR:
Holy Living

MEMORY VERSE: FOR GOD SO LOVED THE WORLD THAT HE GAVE HIS ONE AND ONLY SON, [SO] THAT WHOEVER BELIEVES IN HIM SHALL NOT PERISH BUT HAVE ETERNAL LIFE.

—John 3:16 (NIV; emphasis added)

How are you coming along with your memory verse? This is the first of five verses you will be hiding in your heart. Commit a bit of it to memory each day, and God will be faithful to bless your efforts.

By His grace, Jesus freed us from the law of sin and death. He gave us new life. The next question is, why did He give us this new life?

Read Titus 3:4–8:

But then *something happened*: God our Savior and His overpowering love and kindness for humankind entered our world; He came to save us. It's not that *we earned it* by doing good works or righteous deeds; He came because He is merciful. He brought us *out of our old ways of living* to a new beginning through the washing of regeneration; and He made us completely new through the Holy Spirit, who was poured out in abundance through Jesus the Anointed, our Savior. *All of this happened* **so that** through His grace we would be accepted *into God's covenant family* and appointed to be His heirs, full of the hope that comes from *knowing you have* eternal life. This is a faithful statement *of what we believe*. Concerning this, I want you to put it out there boldly **so that** those who believe in God will be constant in doing the right things, which will benefit all of us. (Bold emphasis added)

living so that 🖋

🖋 Select at least three words in the first sentence that reveal God's grace. Why did you choose these words?

Paul wrote this letter to a young church leader named Titus. He filled it with practical advice to counsel Titus on how to teach God's people to live out their faith in Christian community. In the last verse, Paul advises Titus to give his church a "call to action," a call to holy living.

In the last section, we talked about having new life in Christ. Do the words "new life" intrigue you? Do you long for a new beginning? Do you want to erase the past and start over? I felt that way when we moved to Charlotte many years ago. I wanted to put my past, and all the pain and sorrow that accompanied it, behind me. I wanted a fresh start. I thought moving to a new city would enable me to forget the bad and focus only on the good. But I learned that physical change alone will never accomplish that.

Friend, salvation alone leads to new life . . . a new beginning . . . a fresh start. Paul points this out in the first few verses of Titus 3. At the moment of conversion, God transforms our entire beings, inside and out. He gives us new hearts and new minds. His Holy Spirit changes our desires and inclinations, feelings and emotions, even the motives of our hearts. He renews our minds. We find this same truth written thousands of years before in the book of Ezekiel.

🖋 **Read Ezekiel 36:26–27** and share what the prophet says.

Paul reminds us in Titus 3:4–7 of what God has done for us. God not only declared us righteous (made us right with God) but also justified us. We have new standing in God's eyes. We have been forgiven and found not guilty.

When a judge finds a defendant "not guilty," the court, in essence, declares him innocent. He walks out of the courtroom a free man. God does the very same for us. In spite of all the sins of which we are justly chargeable, He forgives our sins, frees us from the condemnation we deserve, and adopts us into His family . . . making us heirs of eternal life.

We receive this gift for one reason and one reason only: Jesus' perfectly obedient life and His sacrificial death. One moment we are guilty and condemned. The next we are forgiven and free. Read the following passage from Romans:

> Therefore, now no condemnation awaits those who are living in Jesus the Anointed, *the Liberating King,* because when you live in the Anointed One, Jesus, *a new law takes effect.* The law of the Spirit of life *breathes into you and* liberates you from the law of sin and death. God did something the law could never do. *You see, human flesh took its toll on God's law. In and of itself, the law is not weak; but* the flesh weakens it. So to condemn the sin that was *ruling* in the flesh, God sent His own Son, bearing the likeness of sinful flesh, as a sin offering. (Romans 8:1–3)

God credits Jesus' righteousness to us. One moment we are separated from God. The next moment we are reunited with Him, joined together for eternity, never to be separated again. What a precious gift!

I want to say this one more time. Let it sink into the depths of your heart. As unbelievers, we were condemned, guaranteed a life eternally separated from God. As believers, we are saved from that condemnation and given the privilege of spending eternity with our heavenly Father. Hear Paul's words again: "We . . . become heirs having the hope of eternal life" (Titus 3:7 NIV).

Titus 3:4–8, read in its entirety, reveals three beautiful gifts that are ours in Christ:

- a new beginning,

- a new standing, and

- a new future.

Friend, when we dwell on all that God has done for us, how can we *not* "do good" and live our lives in a new and different way?

APPLICATION:

Read Romans 12:1–3.

God's goodness, His generous gift of salvation and new life in Christ, obliges us to live in a new way. The standard is a high one . . . one that seems nearly impossible. His Word says, "Be holy, for I . . . am holy" (Leviticus 19:2). God calls us to holy living. The root of the words translated "holy" and "holiness" is *qadash,* which means "to be set apart or consecrated."[2] Holiness, sweet friend, is our standard. Sound impossible?

Take comfort in these verses:

- I can do everything through him who gives me strength. (Philippians 4:13 NIV)

- You were once at odds *with God*, wicked in your ways and evil in your minds; but now He has reconciled you in His body—in His flesh through His death—**so that** He can present you to God holy, blameless, and *totally* free of imperfection as long as you stay planted in the faith. (Colossians 1:21–23; bold emphasis added)

● By God's will, we are made holy through the offering of the body of Jesus the Anointed once and for all time. (Hebrews 10:10)

When we accept Jesus as our Lord and Savior, He transforms us into new creatures, called and empowered to live by a new standard . . . a standard of holiness.

God directs our every step according to Romans 12:1–2.

Read Romans 12:1–2.

To what are we called in Romans 12:1? Practically, what does this mean?

Once we present ourselves to God, what direction does God give?

It's in the transforming of our minds that we move closer and closer to God's standard of holiness. As ones who are holy and set apart, we are not our own. We belong to God. John Calvin, an influential French theologian and pastor during the Protestant Reformation, wrote:

"We are God's own; to him, therefore, let us live and die. We are God's own; therefore let his wisdom and will dominate all our actions. We are God's own; therefore let every part of our existence be directed towards him as our only legitimate goal."[3]

Holiness becomes a reality when we surrender our hearts and minds to God. We must turn away from our old ways and old habits.

When the urge to return to our old ways rears its ugly head, we must follow God's direction in 2 Corinthians 10:5:

> We demolish arguments and every pretension that sets itself up against the knowledge of God, and we take captive every thought to make it obedient to Christ. (NIV)

🖋 How can we take captive every thought? Give practical examples from your own life.

I struggle with this continually. Just recently, I found myself gossiping. Of course, in the moment I did not call it that. In fact, I justified my words because the person about whom I was talking engaged in behavior that was completely "unchristian." Her actions were judged so by nearly everyone present. We all disapproved. So, in my mind, their words validated my words. It felt good that I was not alone. I took comfort in that.

The next day, as I sat in worship, God spoke to me in a powerful way through the sermon. Our pastor spoke about idle gossip, character assassination, and how words matter. It was as if a sharp knife penetrated my heart.

In the quietness of that moment, I felt conviction. Not guilt. Not shame. But conviction. The difference between these emotions is that guilt and shame are about us and leave us stagnant, in a bad place with God. Conviction, on the other hand, is about God. It's a productive emotion. God's Holy Spirit convicts us to know that we have not pleased Him. He then speaks truth into our hearts and empowers us to change so that we can do what is pleasing to Him.

That day in worship, our pastor shared a verse that spoke directly to my heart. I committed it to memory.

> Don't let even one rotten word seep out of your mouths. Instead, offer only fresh words that build others up when they need it most. That way your good words will communicate grace to those who hear them. (Ephesians 4:29)

Next time, I pray that I will be strong enough to take my words captive *before* they spew forth from my mouth. I pray that I will not speak words that tear down but only words that build up.

GOING DEEPER:

In the event you struggle with holy living, I am including the entire passage on which our pastor taught that day. Read through it. Sit with it awhile and ask the Lord to show you if there is an area in which you are not living according to God's standard of holiness.

Hear the Word of the Lord from Ephesians 4:21–29:

> If you have heard Jesus and have been taught by Him according to the truth that is in Him, then you know to take off your former way of life, your *crumpled* old self—*that dark blot of a soul* corrupted by deceitful desire and lust—*to take a fresh breath* and to let God renew your attitude and spirit. Then *you are ready to* put on your new self, modeled after the very likeness of God: truthful, righteous, and holy.
>
> So put away your lies and speak the truth to one another because we are all part of one another. When you are angry, don't let it carry you into sin. Don't let the sun set with anger in your heart or give the devil room to work. If you have been stealing, stop. Thieves must go to work *like everyone else* and work honestly with their hands **so that** they can share with anyone who has a need. Don't let even one rotten word seep out of your mouths. Instead, offer only fresh words that build others up when they

need it most. That way your good words will communicate grace to those who hear them. (Bold emphasis added)

If God has spoken to you or worked in your heart about this issue or any other, journal your thoughts below and share how you will take action based on what you have heard.

CONCLUDING THOUGHTS:

We have studied another aspect of "so that" living. We spent significant time in God's Word, examining the gift of new life and God's call to holy living. Based on how God has spoken to your heart, complete the thought below.

Jesus came so that . . .

PART FIVE:
Prayer

MEMORY VERSE: FOR GOD SO LOVED THE WORLD THAT HE GAVE HIS ONE AND ONLY SON, **[SO] THAT** WHOEVER BELIEVES IN HIM SHALL NOT PERISH BUT HAVE ETERNAL LIFE.

–John 3:16 (NIV; emphasis added)

We end our chapter studying John 17, one of the longest of Jesus' recorded prayers. The entire prayer contains some of Jesus' most intimate words with His Father in all of Scripture. We open our lesson with the first words of His prayer.

> After Jesus said this, he looked toward heaven and prayed: "Father, the time has come. Glorify your Son, *[so] that* your Son may glorify you. For you granted him authority over all people *[so] that* he might give eternal life to all those you have given him. (John 17:1–2 NIV; emphasis added)

Read Jesus' words as written in *The Voice* and imagine Jesus speaking these words as He lifts His face to the heavens:

> Father, My time has come. Glorify Your Son, and I will bring You great glory because You have given Me total authority over humanity. *I have come bearing the plentiful gifts of God*; and all who receive Me will experience everlasting life, a new intimate relationship with You (the one True God) and Jesus the Anointed (the One You have sent). (John 17:1–2)

In this prayer, Jesus gives us a precious gift, a glimpse into the way He and His Father communicated. Our Savior was a man of prayer. He began His ministry with prayer. Scripture teaches us that He often withdrew to quiet places to pray. And He ended His ministry in prayer in the Garden of Gethsemane. Before we read further, listen to these words from Martin Luther on John 17: "[Jesus] opens the depths of His heart, both in reference to us and to His Father, and He pours them all out. It sounds so honest, so simple. It is so deep, so rich, so wide. No one can fathom it."[4]

APPLICATION:

Let me paint a picture for you. It was the night before His crucifixion. Jesus gathered His closest friends around Him in the Upper Room. During the meal, He humbled Himself before them, showing them the full extent of His love by washing their feet. Why was this significant? Because foot washing was a menial task reserved for the lowliest of servants. By serving them this way, Jesus modeled humility in a way they would never forget.

He then led them on a walk to the Garden of Gethsemane. Jesus knew that the time had come for Him to leave earth and return to heaven. He knew His departure would break His disciples' hearts. They would not understand, so He wanted to prepare them.

In fact, He had just spoken these words of comfort in John 16:33, "I have told you these things so that you will be *whole and* at peace. In this world, you will be plagued with times of trouble, but you need not fear; I have triumphed over this corrupt world order."

Jesus wanted to encourage them.

Jesus wanted to empower them.

So what did He do?

He prayed.

He prayed out loud, in their presence, so they could hear every word.

Read John 17 in its entirety. Soak up every bit of this precious prayer between Jesus and His Abba Father.

We are going to examine the first few verses of this prayer in detail because there is much for us to glean. It's interesting to note that scholars believe Jesus spoke most of the words He shared in John 15–17 as He was "walking along" with His disciples to the Garden of Gethsemane.

John 17:1 says Jesus prayed this prayer *not* with His head bowed but with His eyes lifted "to the heavens."

Why is it significant that Jesus prayed while "walking along" and that His face was lifted "to the heavens"?

I grew up reciting rote prayers with my eyes closed and my head bowed. Jesus broke that mold for me. He was a man of prayer who prayed continually. He prayed in many places and in many ways. His prayers never looked the same. Sometimes He withdrew and prayed alone. Sometimes He prayed in the presence of others. Sometimes He prayed prayers of praise. Sometimes He prayed prayers of desperation. Sometimes He prayed for others. Sometimes He prayed for Himself. Sometimes He prayed early in the morning. Sometimes He prayed in the middle of the day.

Jesus' example teaches us that we can pray whenever and wherever we feel led and called to pray. There are no rules. We can pray silently or out loud. We can pray alone or together. We can pray driving in a car or lying in our beds. We can pray with heads bowed and eyes closed or heads lifted and eyes wide open. What matters most is that you and I become women of prayer. What that looks like is up to us.

🖋 Share what prayer looked like when you were young.

🖋 Share what prayer looks like in your life now.

🖋 Return to John 17 and reread the first few verses. How does Jesus begin His prayer, and for whom is He praying?

I cannot tell you how many times I hear women say they feel bad if they pray for themselves. They think it's selfish. Friend, if you believe this, I want you to know that it's a lie direct from the tongue of the devil! Don't be deceived by the one Jesus calls the father of lies (John 8:44).

Jesus sets the example for us. He opens His prayer in John 17 *first* praying for Himself. Jesus gained strength, power, comfort, and guidance from His Father through prayer. He prayed for His Father to glorify Him so that He, in turn, could glorify His Father in heaven.

If we want to pray for others in powerful and effective ways . . . if we want God to work in and through us for His glory . . . we must first pray for ourselves.

Let's examine what Jesus specifically prays in verse 1:

"Father, the time has come. Glorify your Son, *[so] that* your Son may glorify you." (NIV; emphasis added)

✒ What do you think Jesus meant when He said, "The time has come"?

Do you remember another time when Jesus said similar words about His time?

✒ **Read John 2:3–4.**

Jesus' mother informed Him at the wedding in Cana that the wine supply had run out. Her words implied that she believed that He could do something about it.

✒ Write Jesus' response to His mother. What does it reveal about Jesus and the work He was on earth to do?

> *Jesus' mother informed Him at the wedding in Cana that the wine supply had run out. Her words implied that she believed that He could do something about it.*

His words confound me because they sound almost disrespectful: "Dear woman, is it our problem *they miscalculated when buying wine and inviting guests*? My time has not arrived" (John 2:4).

The King James says, "Woman, what have I to do with thee? mine hour is not yet come."

The second part of His response reveals that He knew there was a time that would come in the future when He would take action. But that time was not now.

When would that time come? It would come three years later. It would be the hour of Christ's redemption, at the end of His long walk of obedience, when His heavenly Father would lavish His love on His created people by sacrificing Jesus on the cross at Calvary. Jesus Christ would willingly give up His own life and shed His own blood for the forgiveness of our sins. God would intentionally separate Himself from His Son for the first and only time to free us from the law of sin and death.

In John 17, that time finally had arrived. Jesus knew this and desperately needed to be close to His Father . . . to be praying for Himself and for those around Him . . . and for us.

What does Jesus ask His Father to do for Him in verse 1? What does this mean?

Jesus was asking His Father to restore Him to His rightful place in heaven. But what had to happen in Jesus' life before His glorious resurrection that Easter morning was unspeakable. The rejection, the shame, the humiliation, the persecution, the torture, the suffering, the suffocation, the death, and the separation were beyond what He could endure alone. Jesus knew He needed His Father to empower Him to live His last hours in a way that would honor and glorify God.

Jesus is glorified so that . . . what?

How does Jesus being glorified glorify His Father?

It is in His death that Jesus glorified the Father, because Jesus' death demonstrated God's great love for His children . . . His selfless, unconditional love.

Write out your memory verse (John 3:16) below.

Jesus had to die so that the reality of God's love for His people could be fully realized.

IF YOU WANT TO GO DEEPER:

Let's examine John 17:1–4, this time from *The Voice*:

> . . . and I will bring You great glory because You have given Me total authority over humanity. *I have come bearing the plentiful gifts of God*; and all who receive Me will experience everlasting life, a new intimate relationship with You (the one True God) and Jesus the Anointed (the One You have sent). I have glorified You on earth and fulfilled the mission You set before Me.

I just love this translation. Scripture teaches here that God has given Jesus authority over all people.

🖋 **Read Matthew 11:27.** Share the truths you learn through Jesus' words.

Here Jesus emphasizes God's absolute sovereignty over all humanity and informs us that God has given that authority to Jesus. When He came to earth, Jesus brought with Him God's richest blessings, and it is only through Jesus that we can receive those blessings. The greatest of those blessings is salvation. And Jesus is very clear: *no one* can be saved apart from God revealing Himself to them, through Jesus.

🖋 **Now read Matthew 11:28.** What does this verse speak to you?

I love how this verse begins. It is a call to action. "Come to Me," it says. "Come to Me, all who are weary and burdened." Jesus calls us to Himself. He is waiting with open arms. "Weary" is a translation of the Greek word *kopiaō*, meaning "to grow weary or exhausted from labour or toil," and "burden" is a translation of the Greek word *photizo*, and refers to one loaded down with a heavy weight.

At one time or another, we are all weary . . . we all carry heavy burdens. There are some of you reading this now who may feel you are collapsing under your heavy load. It may be the burden of sin and its ugly consequences. But it may also be the crushing load we carry because our priorities are not where they should be. We don't know how to say the word *no*. Busyness and overcommitment steal our joy and keep us from fully living in God's peace and rest.

In these Matthew verses, our sweet Jesus offers not only Himself but also His rest. He promises freedom from sin *and* freedom from the toil and troubles of this world. Will you take comfort in these words today? My friend, Jesus' call is not to the strong and sure, but to the weak and the weary.

Will you come to Jesus now? Unload what is burdening your heart in prayer to Him. Sit quietly before Him and truly allow Him to begin to lift your burden. Listen for His voice and write below what you hear.

Jesus died so that you and I could be free from sin and free from all that wearies us and weighs us down. My prayer for you is that you will confidently walk in that freedom today!

CONCLUDING THOUGHTS:

Before we end, I want to encourage you to take time to prayerfully reread John 17 in its entirety. Jesus models prayer for us as He prays for Himself, His disciples, and His church (which is you and me). His heart's desire is that we know Jesus and His Father in a deep and personal way. He doesn't just want us to know the facts . . . that He died, was buried, and rose again. Atheists know the facts. Muslims know the facts. Buddhists know the facts. Agnostics know the facts. Lukewarm Christians know the facts. Jesus wants more for us. He wants us to have a deep and abiding faith in the One on whom those facts are based.

Romans 10:17 says, "Faith comes from hearing the message, and the message is heard through the word of Christ" (NIV). Knowing Jesus intimately comes one way and one way only. We must grow in the grace and knowledge of the Word of God, His love letter to us.

This leads us to our next lesson. But before we leave our first "so that," based on how God has spoken to your heart, complete the thought below.

Jesus came so that...

⇒⟩ MY CALL TO ACTION:

Prayerfully ask the Lord if He has a call to action for you based upon our chapter. If you hear "Yes," write a prayer below asking the Lord to help you obey what you have heard. List a few steps you will take to carry out your call to action.

CHAPTER TWO

God Spoke So That...

MEMORY VERSE: ALL SCRIPTURE IS
GOD-BREATHED AND IS USEFUL FOR
TEACHING, REBUKING, CORRECTING AND
TRAINING IN RIGHTEOUSNESS, **SO THAT**
THE MAN OF GOD MAY BE THOROUGHLY
EQUIPPED FOR EVERY GOOD WORK.

—2 Timothy 3:16–17 (NIV; emphasis added)

⇥⇥ PRAYER:

Join me as we personalize these verses adapted from the
NIV and pray the following truths from God's Word:

Help me not to live on bread alone. (Deuteronomy 8:3)

*Fix these words of Yours on my heart and impress them in my
mind; help me to tie them as symbols on my hands and bind
them on my forehead. Equip me to teach them to my children, talking about them when I sit at home and when I walk*

along the road, when I lie down, and when I get up. (Deuteronomy 6:6–9; 11:18–19)

Help me to keep my way pure by living according to Your Word. (Psalm 119:9)

Make Your Word a lamp to my feet and a light to my path. (Psalm 119:105)

Thank You that Your way is perfect and Your Word is flawless. (2 Samuel 22:31; Proverbs 30:5)

Let Your Word dwell in me richly as I teach and admonish others with all wisdom. (Colossians 3:16)

Help me present myself to You as one approved, a workman who does not need to be ashamed and who correctly handles the Word of Truth. (2 Timothy 2:15)

Help me not merely listen to the Word, and so deceive myself. Enable me to do what it says. (James 1:22)

When Your words come, help me to eat them and digest them. Make them my joy and my heart's delight. (Jeremiah 15:16)

Thank You that though heaven and earth will pass away, Your words will never pass away. (Matthew 24:35)

PART ONE:
The Word

Hours of prayer and study reside within the pages of the book you hold in your hand today. God has called me to teach His Word, and I absolutely love it! It's my joy and privilege to walk beside you and break apart God's Word together. We study the Bible to understand the heart of the One who wrote it and to learn how to practically apply it in our lives. The study of God's Word is imperative in the life of every believer, and I would not continue teaching if I didn't believe that what we are doing has great purpose. Let's look at several key passages of Scripture that teach this very truth.

Read 2 Timothy 3:16–17, this week's memory verse. Why does Paul say God has given us the written Word?

Read Romans 15:4:

> For everything that was written in the past was written to teach us, *[so] that* through endurance and the encouragement of the Scriptures we might have hope. (NIV; emphasis added)

What does Paul add here?

🖋 <u>Read 1 Corinthians 10:6, 11</u> and share another purpose of God's written Word.

God breathed the very depths of His heart into the hearts and minds of generations of men and women. He interacted with them over thousands of years not only to teach us about our past but also to instruct us on how to live for the future. He wants us to avoid making the same mistakes and suffering the same consequences they did.

⟫ APPLICATION:

We are going to spend significant time today in 2 Timothy 3:16–17:

> All Scripture is God-breathed and is useful for teaching, rebuking, correcting and training in righteousness, *so that* the man of God may be thoroughly equipped for every good work. (NIV; emphasis added)

In these verses, Paul was speaking to a young man he was mentoring named Timothy. Paul wrote two letters to Timothy (namely, 1 and 2 Timothy) to equip him to care for and instruct the church Paul had established in Ephesus.

Paul knew Timothy was young and might feel a bit intimidated to step into his shoes. So just prior to these verses, Paul reminded Timothy of the legacy left him by his mother and grandmother (2 Timothy 3:14–15). Timothy had been taught the holy Scriptures from the time he was a young child by people who loved him dearly and in whom he had great trust. Paul wanted to leave Timothy with words that would help him begin his ministry from a place of faith and confidence.

Paul used the word "holy" to remind Timothy that the Scriptures with which he was entrusted were not just any writings. They were sacred and holy. "Holy" means "set apart by God for special use." This is something we should always remember. God's Word is sacred and should be treated as such.

A story is told about Dr. David Livingstone, a Scottish missionary in Africa who lived in the 1800s. Reading was one of his greatest passions.

On one of his long treks through the African jungle, he insisted on taking his most prized books. He asked the members of his mission team to help him carry seventy-three books weighing 180 pounds! After three hundred miles, he realized what he had asked of them was unreasonable. They began dropping books along the way until there was only one remaining . . . his Bible. He refused to part with it. He treasured God's Word and was quoted as saying, "All that I am I owe to Jesus Christ, revealed to me in His divine Book."[1]

What a powerful illustration of how one man treasured God's Word above all other possessions. Oh, that we would all treasure God's Word this way!

How do you view the Word of God? Do you treasure it? If so, how do you express your attitude toward His Word?

With regard to the sacredness of the Word, some people contend that if we carry a stack of books, our Bibles should always be on top. Others say we should never place our Bibles on the floor.

God's Word is sacred and should be treated as such.

And still others say that we should never set anything on top of our Bibles (coffee cup, dessert plate, etc.). What do you think? Is that a little over the top?

Now let's return to 2 Timothy 3:16. Paul states very clearly, "All Scripture is God-breathed." The King James Version says, "All scripture is given by inspiration of God."

First, note it says, "All Scripture." At the time Paul wrote this letter, the entirety of the Old Testament and many of the New Testament books had been written. So when he wrote, "All Scripture," he was not referring solely to the Old Testament. He intentionally used the word "all" so his audience would know he meant the Old *and* the New Testaments are God-breathed.

By using the words "God-breathed," Paul affirmed God's active involvement in the writing of the holy Scriptures. The phrase "God-breathed" is actually a very literal translation of the Greek word *theopneustos,* from the root words *theos* (God) and *pneuma* (breath). Friend, this truth is vital to our study of God's Word. It means that *every* word of Scripture you and I read is God-inspired. The words are God's, not man's. God's Spirit penetrated the hearts and minds of each writer in such a powerful and pervasive way that it makes the words he wrote infallible and authoritative.

2 Peter 1:20–21 confirms this:

> But notice first that no prophecy found in Scripture is a matter of the prophet's own interpretation. Prophecy has never been a product of human initiative, but it comes when men *and women* are moved to speak on behalf of God by the Holy Spirit.

Our God is a God of truth:

> He is the Rock, his work is perfect: for all his ways are judgment: a *God of truth* and without iniquity, just and right is he. (Deuteronomy 32:4 KJV; emphasis added)

[Jesus said] I am the path, **the truth**, and the *energy of* life. No one comes to the Father except through Me. (John 14:6; bold emphasis added)

Jesus the Anointed is the One who came by water and blood—not by the water only, but by the water and the blood . . . The Spirit of God testifies to this **truth** because the Spirit is the **truth**. (1 John 5:6; bold emphasis added)

And of the Scriptures themselves, Jesus says, "Thy word is *truth*" (John 17:17 KJV; emphasis added).

Each writer had his own style, personality, and vocabulary, giving each book a different feel and a different voice. Each one approached writing from his circumstances, his heart, and his perspective. Yet each, as he wrote, was under the supernatural influence of the Holy Spirit. And this guarantees that what each one wrote is accurate and trustworthy. God and man worked in tandem, with God being the ultimate source of every written word.

Do you believe the Bible is the inspired Word of God? If you answered no, what do you believe about the Bible and its accuracy and authenticity?

The second half of 2 Timothy 3:16 tells us that God's Word is "profitable" (KJV), meaning it is useful for our lives.

🖋 List the four reasons Paul gives for God's Word being "profitable." Explain how each applies in your life.

Finally, Paul ends with verse 17, telling Timothy that God uses His Word to prepare and equip His people for service. The King James Version says, "That the man of God may be perfect, thoroughly furnished unto all good works."

"Perfect" is a translation of the Greek word *artios* and refers "not only to the presence of all the parts that are necessary for completeness but also to the further adaptation and aptitude of those parts for their designed purpose." Please know that "perfect" as used here does not at all suggest sinless perfection. Rather, it implies being fitted for the use for which God created us. God uses His Word to perfectly equip us for the purpose for which He created us.

> The better you and I know the Word, the better able we are to live out God's plan for our lives.

"Furnished" is a translation of the Greek word *exartizo* and means "to complete" or "to equip." God gives us exactly what we need to accomplish the tasks He purposed for us to do. The Word of God equips us so that we can live the life God planned for us before time began.

What is the logical conclusion? The better you and I know the Word, the better able we are to live out God's plan for our lives.

Yes, we study the Bible to learn history. Yes, we read the Bible to learn doctrine. Yes, we examine the Bible to know how to defend our faith. But, my friend, one of the most important reasons we read the Word is to equip us . . . first with salvation and then with all we need to do the work of God. The Bible equips us for ministry. And ministry is not limited to pastors, priests, nuns, speakers, authors, and Bible teachers. Ministry is doing God's work wherever He has placed us . . . in our home, in our school, in our workplace, in our neighborhood, in our community, and in our world.

Share how God has used His Word to prepare and equip you in your own life.

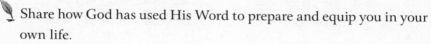

CONCLUDING THOUGHTS:

You have spent time digging into the words Paul wrote to Timothy. You have studied much about our second "so that." Based on how God has spoken to your heart, complete the thought below.

God spoke so that . . .

PART TWO:
Established in the Truth

MEMORY VERSE: ALL SCRIPTURE IS GOD-BREATHED AND
IS USEFUL FOR TEACHING, REBUKING, CORRECTING AND
TRAINING IN RIGHTEOUSNESS, **SO THAT** THE MAN OF GOD MAY
BE THOROUGHLY EQUIPPED FOR EVERY GOOD WORK.

–2 Timothy 3:16–17 (NIV; emphasis added)

⤞ APPLICATION:

Paul, the most prolific writer of the New Testament, wrote the book
of Romans to present the gospel message to the people of Rome. He
wanted to establish a strong church in Rome, and, to accomplish
that, he had to ensure they understood the fundamental truths of
the gospel. Accordingly, in Romans, Paul set forth a road map to
explain God's plan of salvation.

Read this passage from Romans 16:

So to the One who is able to strengthen you to live consistently
with my good news and the preaching of Jesus, the Anointed,
with the revelation of the ancient mystery that has been kept
secret since the earliest days, this mystery is revealed through
the prophetic voices passed down in the Scriptures, as they have
been commanded by the Eternal God. *In this time,* this mystery
is being made known to the nations **so that** all may be led to
faith-filled obedience. (Romans 16:25–26; bold emphasis added)

Paul begins this passage stating, "So to *the One* who is able to
strengthen . . ." "The One" refers to God. Although Paul was the
messenger, he recognized that it was God who would do the work.
God is the One who strengthens our faith. The word "strengthen"
here—translated "establish" in the NIV—is a translation of the

Greek word *sterizo*, which means "to make something firm or stable; to make it fast." It occurs several times in the New Testament and pertains to something being settled both spiritually and mentally in the truth of God's Word. It incorporates not only our hearts but also our minds. Being established in the Word is a prerequisite to having strong, firm, and immovable faith.

How can we become established in the Word? What are some mistakes people make as they try to establish themselves in God's Word?

Colossians 2:7 in the New Living Translation reads:

> Let your roots grow down into him, and let your lives be built on him. Then your faith will grow strong in the truth you were taught, and you will overflow with thankfulness.

The key to establishing our faith is spending time in God's Word. We can't accomplish it by attending worship once a week, by periodically participating in Bible studies, or by watching a televangelist on Sunday mornings. We must commit to reading and studying God's Word for ourselves. It is only when we read and meditate on His Word that God will establish His "living and active" (Hebrews 4:12 NIV) Word in us in a way that cultivates deep roots that eventually transform our hearts and minds, or our inner man. And, friend, when we are firmly established in our inner man . . . our spirits (how we think and pray), we will be steadfast in our outer man . . . our flesh (how we feel and act).

My prayer is that as we work through this week's lessons, God will grow in each of us a deep desire to become established in His truth.

🖋 **Read Philippians 1:4–6** and share how 2 Timothy 3:16 (from yesterday's lesson) and our Romans verse from today's lesson all work together.

Let's revisit our Romans passage (chapter 16), this time focusing on verses 25–26. Paul explains how the gospel message had been a "mystery" (NIV) for many years. When I see the word "mystery," it always makes me think of one of my favorite old television shows, *Murder, She Wrote*. Week after week, Jessica Fletcher solved mysteries not only in her tiny hometown of Cabot Cove, but also in exciting cities across the globe. *Murder, She Wrote* began with a murder, but the identity of the murderer remained a mystery throughout the show. The truth was not revealed until Jessica, in her genius, solved the clues and revealed the culprit!

A mystery is not something unknowable. Rather, the term refers to something real that has been hidden. So, "mystery" as used in Romans 16 "refers to part of the revelation of Almighty God that was not known in the Old Testament, but has become known in the New."[3] To know the mystery requires divine revelation. God, not Jessica Fletcher, decides when, how, and through whom it will be made known.

We see this revelation of mystery clearly played out in the book of Hebrews. God hid many New Testament truths in shadows, figures, rituals, and types throughout the Old Testament, and it wasn't until the birth of Jesus that God brought understanding to these mysteries. God revealed them to the author of Hebrews. Chapter by chapter He unfolded each and every type and revealed how it pointed to Christ.

Friend, we are so blessed to live in New Testament times, blessed to be the beneficiaries of God's New Testament revelations. What was once hidden is now revealed. And Paul knows that God commissioned him as one of the very first men to reveal all that had been hidden. Can you imagine what it must have felt like for him? Can you feel the great responsibility he carried to make God's revelations known?

 God commissioned Paul to reveal the mystery "so that" what?

IF YOU WANT TO GO DEEPER:

God's deepest longing is for His creation to know Him, love Him, believe Him, and obey Him. He entrusted Paul with this privilege of making God known. In fact, Paul was the first to share the gospel message outside the community of God's chosen people, the Jews. God specially called him to bring the gospel to the Gentiles (non-Jews).

Read Ephesians 3:8–11. List some key truths you learn in this passage. For example,

1. What does verse 8 reveal about Paul?

2. According to verses 8–9, what was Paul's call?

3. What was God's purpose? (v. 10)

4. Through whom did God carry out this plan? (v. 11)

Read 1 Corinthians 15:9 and 1 Timothy 1:15–16.

1. What do these verses teach you about Paul?

2. What do these verses teach you about the kind of person God chooses to preach His Word?

3. Why would God choose this sort of person?

CONCLUDING THOUGHTS:

As we close our lesson, it's clear that God revealed the mystery of the gospel because He wanted all the nations of the world to believe and obey Christ. Jesus' last words to His disciples speak to the truth of this statement: "Therefore, go and make disciples of all the nations, baptizing them in the name of the Father and the Son and the Holy Spirit" (Matthew 28:19 NLT).

This call to spread the gospel did not end with the disciples. We, too, are called to go and make disciples of all nations. But the spreading of the gospel will never occur, let alone be effective, without people who have a deeply rooted faith, firmly established in the Word. Paul understood the truth of that statement and, through Romans and his other letters, sought to instill it in Timothy, in the church, and in each one of us.

You have spent significant time with the words of Paul. Based on what you have learned, complete the "so that" below.

God spoke so that . . .

PART THREE:
The Word as Spoken Through Luke

MEMORY VERSE: ALL SCRIPTURE IS GOD-BREATHED AND
IS USEFUL FOR TEACHING, REBUKING, CORRECTING AND
TRAINING IN RIGHTEOUSNESS, **SO THAT** THE MAN OF GOD MAY
BE THOROUGHLY EQUIPPED FOR EVERY GOOD WORK.

-2 Timothy 3:16-17 (NIV; emphasis added)

I pray you are hiding this beautiful verse in your heart. Whenever you doubt a promise or a truth because of something going on in your life, ask the Lord to bring this verse to mind. He will use it to comfort you and remind you that His Word is truth, written for you today, to speak specifically into your life and your circumstances.

Today we will spend time in the gospel of Luke. If you have never met him, allow me to introduce you. Luke was not among the twelve disciples. In fact, it is believed that he was Greek, making him a Gentile by birth. Paul fondly referred to Luke as "the beloved physician" in Colossians 4:14 (ESV). Luke was not only a highly educated man but also a great historian.

In addition to being a doctor, Luke was a missionary. Many credit Paul for bringing Luke to faith during one of his missionary journeys. After becoming a believer, Luke accompanied Paul on many of his travels. Scholars believe Luke wrote his gospel and the book of Acts while with Paul in Rome during Paul's first Roman imprisonment.[4] Luke wrote mainly to Gentiles and Christians to strengthen and encourage them in their faith.

Luke never married, but served the Lord throughout his life until he died at age eighty-four.[5]

Read Luke 1:1–3. To whom did Luke write his gospel, and why?

Each of the gospel writers relays the events surrounding Jesus' birth, ministry, and death in his own way. Luke states his method and purpose up front. His gospel presents a carefully investigated, chronological, orderly account of Jesus' life and ministry. The lawyer in me identifies with his gospel the most! And although his gospel differs from the others in many ways, Luke did not write his gospel to challenge the other gospel writers. He loved history, enjoyed research, and, accordingly, wrote his gospel to present a more detailed account of Jesus' life and ministry.

APPLICATION:

Some of Jesus' best-known parables appear in Luke. Today we will study a familiar parable that is one of my favorites. If you have read it or studied it before, I invite you to ask the Lord to help you read it with fresh eyes.

Read Luke 8:4–15. Our "so that" is found in verses 9–10:

> His disciples asked him what this parable meant. He said, "The knowledge of the secrets of the kingdom of God has been given to you, but to others I speak in parables, *so that,*
>
>> 'though seeing, they may not see;
>> though hearing, they may not understand.'" (NIV; emphasis added)

A parable is a short story with a double meaning. Another way to define a parable would be an earthly story with a heavenly meaning.

Jesus told His disciples there are "secrets" of the kingdom of God that not everyone knows. Luke 8:10 tells us that Jesus revealed those secrets to a chosen few, and His twelve disciples were among those chosen few.

Don't you love to know a secret? I feel really special when a friend entrusts me with her secret. That is what Jesus' words imply here. Because His disciples were special, He entrusted them with kingdom secrets. The word for "secret" as used here is *musterion* and refers to a "sacred thing hidden which is naturally unknown to human reason and is only known by the revelation of God."

Sound familiar? We just studied a similar concept in our last section when we studied the word "mystery."

> Jesus wants to take us deeper still with Him into His Word, and all we need to do is ask!

Friend, I want you to be encouraged because the secrets Jesus disclosed were not reserved for only the Twelve. John 8:31 tells us that when we hold to Jesus' teachings, we, too, are His disciples. And just as He shared the secrets of His kingdom with His twelve disciples, He longs to share those same secrets with us. He wants to take us deeper still with Him into His Word, and all we need to do is ask!

In Matthew 13 (where we also find this same parable) we read that Jesus taught this parable from a boat. I often wonder if Jesus was teaching from what He observed around Him. Perhaps He watched people walking toward Him on a well-worn footpath. Maybe surrounding that footpath, He saw rocky crags jutting out of barren soil and ground overridden by thornbushes. As He looked beyond the crowd, in the distance, maybe He saw a field yielding rich crops. And it was these observations that brought the parable alive and gave it value and meaning to His audience.

With this visual in mind, let's dig into Luke's parable.

In Jesus' time, farmers planted seed by hand. In this story, as the farmer scattered the seeds, they traveled to four locations in his field. Some fell along a dirt path. People continually traveled this path, causing the soil to be packed down hard. Consequently, when the seed landed on this impenetrable soil, it would simply lie on top until the birds came and ate it.

Some seed fell among the rock. This refers not to a pile of rocks but rather a place where a thin layer of soil covered a rocky ledge. So there was enough soil for the seed to take root, but its roots could not go deep. Thus, they received no nourishment and soon withered and died.

Other seed fell among thorns. The good seed took root, but it grew up alongside thorns. The thorns grew faster and overtook the good seed and choked out the very life they produced.

Finally, some seed fell in rich, good soil. It was this seed, Luke says, that produced a crop that was "a hundred times as much as had been planted" (v. 8 NLT).

When Jesus finished the parable, His disciples were confused. Before He explained it, what did Jesus say at the end of verse 8? What do you think Jesus meant by these words?

Jesus' words confused the disciples. They heard but did not understand, so they asked Jesus what He meant. He replied with the "so that" passage we opened with today:

> "The knowledge of the secrets of the kingdom of God has been given to you, but to others I speak in parables, *so that*,
>
>> 'though seeing, they may not see;
>> though hearing, they may not understand.'" (v. 10 NIV; emphasis added)

living so that ◄◄

The New Living Translation says, "You are permitted to understand the secrets of the Kingdom of God . . ."

🖋 Was Jesus really speaking in parables to *hide* the kingdom from "others," from those outside His circle? Explain.

It does not seem fair, but that is what Jesus appears to say. What we can infer from Jesus' words is that He was looking for "listening ears." When we have listening ears, we will hear *and* understand. Jesus purposely spoke in parables to distinguish between those who had "ears to hear" (those with responsive hearts) and those who did not. His words in verses 8 and 10 imply an element of accountability.

The Old Testament reference in verse 10 is from Isaiah 6, where God tells His prophet Isaiah this same truth. Isaiah would preach God's message, but because of the people's hardened hearts, they would hear and not understand; they would see and not comprehend. God cannot work in the lives of those who have hardened hearts. Their eyes and ears are not open and available to really listen and understand what He has to say.

Jesus' parables are vehicles of revelation to those who hunger for and desire to know truth. Stubborn, rebellious, arrogant, doubting, hardened hearts may hear, but they will never understand. Is God Himself responsible? In a sense, yes, because "listening ears" are a prerequisite to hearing and understanding His message. But the reality is that the fault lies with man. Scripture lays out exactly how we come to know and

> When we have listening ears, we will hear and understand.

recognize the voice of God, but the majority of people choose to ignore it.

Now let's open our ears so we can hear the truths Jesus wants us to glean from this parable.

Who is the sower? Can there be more than one sower?

The sower may refer to the Son of Man, but it can also refer to anyone who preaches and teaches the Word of God.

What does the seed represent?

What does the soil represent?

When we accept Jesus as our Lord and Savior, we each receive a new heart, one that can perceive and understand the things of God (Ezekiel 36:26–27). Proverbs 4:23 says we should guard our hearts because they are the wellsprings of life (NIV). Matthew teaches that where our treasure is, there our hearts will be also (Matthew 6:21).

Friend, God's Word makes it very clear that the state of our hearts determines the quality of our "listening ears."

Jesus speaks of four types of soil, each one representing the heart of one who reads or hears the Word of God. Take a moment and dissect each soil type as it relates to the heart, and explain why that impacts the heart's ability to receive the message.

1. Path

2. Rocky ground

3. Thorns

4. Good soil

The seed along the path represents people who hear the Word, but it has no place to go. Their hearts are hardened, so Satan comes and snatches the seed away.

The seed on the rocky soil represents those who have a shallow faith. They actually receive the Word with joy but never allow it to penetrate their hearts and minds, thus it never takes root. When a time of testing comes, there is nothing to keep them grounded in their faith, so they fall away.

The seed that fell among the thorns represents those who hear and receive the Word, but their hearts are so distracted by the things of the world that they choke out what they have heard. They never mature in their faith. We must be so careful because our hearts can produce both thorns and fruit. But one *will* win out over the other. In a heart filled with thorns, the thorns choke out the fruit and leave the heart empty and unsatisfied, always seeking but never finding.

The seed that fell on good soil represents those who have noble and good hearts. They not only hear and receive the Word; they retain it. It takes root, and the roots go deep. These hearts obey and persevere, so much so that God blesses that perseverance and obedience and causes their hearts to produce a great harvest. Their lives produce abundant fruit that brings glory, honor, and praise to God.

Examine your heart and prayerfully consider which soil represents your heart. Share what you discover. Do you think the "soil" of our hearts can be changed? If so, how?

> We must be so careful because our hearts can produce both thorns and fruit.

CONCLUDING THOUGHTS:

Luke uses the word "hear" at least seven times in this passage. Why? Because having ears to hear is *key* to understanding the Word of God and growing deeper in our faith. Romans 10:17 says faith comes by hearing the Word of God.

Luke likens the Word to seed because, like a seed, it is living and active. It takes root. And its purpose, once it takes root in our hearts, is to produce fruit. In order for it to produce fruit, it must be watered and fertilized.

This growth process cannot begin without "listening ears." Don't you want to be a woman with whom Christ can share the secrets of His kingdom? Friend, during our lifetime, we barely scratch the surface of the riches God has for us in His Word. But His desire is that we receive every bit of those riches that we are humanly able to receive. Don't let the things of this world get in the way and choke out your ability to receive the full riches of God's treasures.

As we close today, remember that *all* four hearts in the parable heard the Word. Yet only *one* produced a harvest. God declared in Isaiah 55:11 that His Word will not return void (KJV) but will accomplish what He desires and achieve the purposes for which He sent it. But for it to be effective in us, that seed, His Word, requires fertile soil. Oh, sweet friend, my prayer is that as we grow together in and through this study, God will find fertile soil in each one of our hearts.

Is your soil fertile? Is your heart ready to receive the Word? Once received, is your heart prepared . . . free from the cares of this world so that God's Word can take root? If yes, share evidence of it taking root. If not, what do you need to do to allow it to take root?

If the Word has taken root in your heart, is it producing fruit? If yes, share some fruit you have seen produced. If not, what are steps you can take to water and fertilize your heart so that the Word in you will produce fruit?

We have spent time carefully studying Luke's parable of the sower. Based on what you have learned, complete the "so that" below.

God spoke so that . . .

PART FOUR:
The Word as Spoken Through John

MEMORY VERSE: ALL SCRIPTURE IS GOD-BREATHED AND
IS USEFUL FOR TEACHING, REBUKING, CORRECTING AND
TRAINING IN RIGHTEOUSNESS, **SO THAT** THE MAN OF GOD MAY
BE THOROUGHLY EQUIPPED FOR EVERY GOOD WORK.

–2 Timothy 3:16–17 (NIV; emphasis added)

In this section we will spend time with John, also known as "the disciple Jesus loved" (John 13:23 NLT). What is so intriguing about this statement is that John alone called himself by this name. At first, it makes him sound a bit arrogant. But as you read through John's writings, you will sense that it is more likely that John experienced God's love in such powerful ways that he knew without a doubt Jesus chose him, called him, and deeply loved him. He knew his identity was in Christ, and, because of that, he knew he was the Lord's beloved.

Oh, that we would have that confidence to unabashedly speak those same words: "I am the girl Jesus loves!" No matter my actions, no matter my words, no matter my mistakes, no matter my exploding emotions, "I am the girl Jesus loves!"

Like Luke, John had a definite purpose for writing his gospel. Interestingly, his gospel contains very little content that we find in the other gospels because his expressed purpose was to prove the absolute deity of Jesus. Like no other New Testament writer, John presents Jesus as the Son of God. He knew that the salvation of his audience could not be secured without the firm belief that Jesus was the Son of God. John desired for every person to have an intimate, personal, eternal relationship with Jesus and makes this very clear in the last chapter when he writes:

Jesus performed many other wondrous signs that are not written in this book. These accounts are recorded **so that** you, too, might believe that Jesus is the Anointed, *the Liberating King,* the Son of God, because believing grants you the life He came to share. (John 20:30–31; bold emphasis added)

John carefully chose his stories to teach his audience that the One about whom he was writing was none other than God Himself, clothed in human flesh. Like no other gospel writer, John teaches us about the character of God. He uses the daily interactions of people with Jesus to reveal God's character through His names . . . the Bread of Life; the Light of the World; the Good Shepherd; the Resurrection and the Life; the Way, the Truth, and the Life; and the True Vine.

As we begin our lesson today, keep in mind the word "believe." Count how many times you find it in our readings. Consider how it is used. John teaches us a subtle distinction. We can believe *in* Christ and we can believe Christ. Believing *in* Christ is the first step of faith and leads us to salvation. But *believing* Christ is an ongoing activity and requires a relationship. In the midst of our everyday living, we must believe Christ for who He is and what He promises He will do. Even when our circumstances scream otherwise because our physical eyes cannot see and our emotions cannot feel, we must believe. Even when all seems hopeless, we must believe.

Let's dig in to see what John has for us today.

APPLICATION:

As we read through John's gospel, time and time again we find phrases like this: "I tell you," "I have told you in advance," and

In the midst of our everyday living, we must believe Christ for who He is and what He promises He will do.

"I have told you these things." Read the following examples and answer the questions. Also note that each one contains a "so that."

Read John 13:19 and John 14:29, quoted below:

> "Assuredly, I tell you these truths before they happen **so that** when it all transpires, you will believe that I am." (John 13:19; bold emphasis added)

1. What is Jesus telling them now? (For more insight read John 13:18–30.)

2. Why is He telling them?

3. Why is strengthening their belief so important?

The disciples' assignment after Jesus' death would be to continue the work He had been doing. Jesus knew that, as it stood, they were not strong enough to take on such a monumental assignment. He needed to fortify their faith. So the fact that Jesus knew of Judas's betrayal and spoke of it in advance bolstered the disciples' faith. Jesus used many "so that" statements like this to continually build their faith.

"I have told you all these things in advance **so that** your faith will grow as these things come to pass." (John 14:29; bold emphasis added)

1. What is Jesus telling them before it happens? (For more insight read Mark 8:31; 9:31–32; John 14:15–18, 28–31.)

2. Why would strengthening their belief in preparation for that moment in His ministry be imperative?

Jesus needed His disciples to know that although He would be absent physically, He would not be gone altogether. He made them a powerful promise in these verses. They would still experience His presence even though they would not see or sense Him physically.

I'm certain that at the time Jesus spoke these words, they did not understand, but imagine how comforting the following words were to them after His death:

"I will ask the Father to send you another Helper, *the Spirit of truth*, who will remain constantly with you. The world does not recognize the Spirit of truth, because it does not know the Spirit and is unable to receive Him. But you do know the Spirit because He lives with you, and He will dwell in you. I will never abandon you like orphans; I will return to be with you." (John 14:16–18)

Does it sometimes feel as if you can't hear God? Does He seem distant? Jesus wants us to know that even when we feel this way, He is not absent. He is not distant. He is with us. He is always available.

God promises this in Jeremiah 29:12–14: "'At that time, you will call out for Me, *and I will hear*. You will pray, and I will listen. You will look for Me intently, and you will find Me. *Yes*, I will be found by you,' says the Eternal."

His Spirit indwells us. When we tap into that Spirit by spending time in His Word and in prayer, we experience His presence. And when we experience His presence, belief becomes so much easier.

Recently my daughter texted me and asked for prayer. She is a sophomore in college and had an economics exam about which she was extremely nervous. I texted back a quick prayer. A few minutes later, the Lord prompted me to send her a verse, Proverbs 3:5–6. As I sent it, I prayed that He would encourage her and build her confidence through the verse. The next morning I awakened to a text from Lauren that read:

> I opened my devotional for today and today's truth was Proverbs 3:5, exactly the verse you gave me last night!! Encouragement!

Do you see how the process works? First, I had God's Word hidden in my heart. My daughter asked for prayer in her time of need. I texted back a prayer. God kept her request on my heart and a short while later prompted me to send her another text with a verse. At the time, I knew neither the devotional nor the verse she would read the next morning, but God did. So He reminded me of that particular verse, which was hidden in my heart, and prompted me to send it, which I did. I sent it with a silent prayer asking for Him to use it to encourage her. She read it the next morning, and the very word she used to describe what it meant was "Encouragement!"

Lauren walked into her test with a peace that she never would have had but for God's work in her heart and mind during the previous twelve hours. It's a peace that the world cannot give. It's a gift from God.

What do we learn from this story? The more we say yes to spending time with God in His Word, the more we will recognize His voice. The more we recognize His voice, the more we will live in expectation of seeing Him at work. The more we see God at work, the more we will experience Him in our midst. And the more we experience Him, the more we will be able to trust Him in all things. It all starts with saying yes to God's invitation to meet with Him.

Let's end today's lesson going a bit deeper into God's precious gift of peace.

> "I have told you these things **so that** you will be *whole and* at peace. In this world, you will be plagued with times of trouble, but you need not fear; I have triumphed over this corrupt world order." (John 16:33; bold emphasis added)

Jesus begins by saying, "I have told you these things." Define "these things" (read John 16).

In John 14 and 15, Jesus comforted His disciples with life-sustaining words. In chapter 16, Jesus continued with some of His most encouraging words yet. For context, this verse comes just after He spoke the following words:

The more we say yes to spending time with God in His Word, the more we will recognize His voice.

"So you believe now? Be aware that a time is coming when you will be scattered *like seeds*. You will return to your own way, and I will be left alone. But I will not be alone, because the Father will be with Me." (John 16:31–32)

and just before Jesus' beautiful prayer we studied earlier, in John 17.

In whom do we have peace? How is that possible?

What does it mean to "have peace" in Christ? How does God's peace manifest itself?

Practically, how do we live in the fullness of God's peace?

Jesus knew that His death would create great despair in the hearts of His followers. For three years they had followed Him and lived nearly every moment with Him. He was their teacher, their leader, and their friend. He led them and fed them. He prayed for them and cared for them. They loved Him deeply.

Because of this, people identified them with Jesus. Jesus knew their lives were at risk because of their friendship with Him. He knew they were afraid of persecution and even death because they were His followers. Jesus knew He needed to speak hope into their lives to assure them that even though they would have trouble after He was gone, they should not be anxious or afraid. He had a gift for them . . . a gift of peace . . . but not just any peace, an everlasting peace that no one could take away.

How is peace like that possible? Because of the Holy Spirit. After His death and resurrection, Jesus physically left this earth to take His rightful place in heaven, seated at the right hand of His Father. He left our world physically, but He did not leave His people alone. He came back to join them in the person of the Holy Spirit. It began with Pentecost and His disciples and continues to this day for all who believe in Him as their Lord and Savior. Through God's Holy Spirit, we are connected with Jesus for eternity!

We encounter Him every time we open His living and active Word. We connect with Him every time we come before His throne of grace in prayer. And He promises that when we come, He will hear us.

Jesus encouraged His disciples and encourages us that though we will have trouble in this world, He has overcome the world! Through His Spirit, we will find peace in times of pressure and uncertainty, in times of fear and waiting. He is the Prince of Peace (Isaiah 9:6), and His peace reigns. John 14:27 tells us that His peace is not the peace the world gives.

Distinguish between the world's peace and the peace of Jesus.

Through God's Holy Spirit, we are connected with Jesus for eternity!

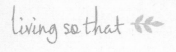 *living so that*

 Read Philippians 4:6–7. How do we secure Jesus' peace in our lives?

>> IF YOU WANT TO GO DEEPER:

 Here are a few more "so that" verses found in the gospel of John. Take some time to sit with these verses and share what you learn from each one and John's purpose in using it.

> "I have told you this *so that* my joy may be in you and that your joy may be complete." (John 15:11 NIV; emphasis added)

> "All this [what I said in chapter 15] I have told you *so that* you will not go astray." (John 16:1 NIV; emphasis added)

> "None has been lost except the one doomed to destruction [Judas] *so that* Scripture would be fulfilled." (John 17:12 NIV; emphasis added)

This happened [Jesus being handed over to the Romans] *so that* the words Jesus had spoken indicating the kind of death he was going to die [crucifixion*] would be fulfilled. (John 18:32 NIV; emphasis added; see also John 12:32–33)

Later, knowing that all was now completed, and *so that* the Scripture would be fulfilled, Jesus said, "I am thirsty." (John 19:28 NIV; emphasis added; see Psalm 69:21)

This testimony is true. In fact, it is an eyewitness account; and he has reported what he saw **so that** you also may believe. It happened this way to fulfill the Hebrew Scriptures that "not one of His bones shall be broken"; and the Hebrew Scriptures also say, "They will look upon Him whom they pierced." (John 19:35–37; bold emphasis added; see also Psalm 34:20; Zechariah 12:10)

---

* Note: Jewish execution was by stoning, but Jesus' death was to be by crucifixion. The Roman execution was by crucifixion, so the Romans, not the Jews, had to be the ones to put Jesus to death.

living so that ⟨⟨⟨

⟩⟩ CONCLUDING THOUGHTS:

We have spent precious time with John, the disciple Jesus loved. He filled his gospel with a multitude of "so that" verses. Based on what you have learned, complete the "so that" below.

God spoke so that . . .

PART FIVE:
The Word as Spoken Through Paul

MEMORY VERSE: ALL SCRIPTURE IS GOD-BREATHED AND
IS USEFUL FOR TEACHING, REBUKING, CORRECTING AND
TRAINING IN RIGHTEOUSNESS, **SO THAT** THE MAN OF GOD MAY
BE THOROUGHLY EQUIPPED FOR EVERY GOOD WORK.

–2 Timothy 3:16–17 (NIV; emphasis added)

What a study this has been so far. We have traveled all over
Scripture and examined the words of many of God's greatest leaders and teachers. Can you believe how many "so that" verses we
have found, and we have not even scratched the surface? Have you
enjoyed examining the "so thats" of God's spoken Word? Today we
spend time again in the words of Paul.

God's Word is our contact with Him. It's how
we hear His voice, discover His direction, receive
His correction, and obtain His hope. He promises
that when His Word goes out, it will not return
void (Isaiah 55:11 KJV). He promises that it will
be health to our bodies and nourishment to our
bones (Proverbs 3:8 NIV; see also Proverbs 4:20–
22). He promises that in and through it, He will
show us great and mighty things (Jeremiah 33:3).
In fact, in Matthew 4:4 (the temptation of Jesus),
Jesus says that we are to live and be sustained by
every Word that comes from the mouth of God.

Jesus says that we are to live and be sustained by every Word that comes from the mouth of God.

My prayer is that after you spend time steeped
in the "so thats," they will take root in our hearts.
Once they take root, they will invade our minds

and come alive in us. They will drive our choices, actions, and reactions in the midst of our messy lives.

Over time, they will form on our tongues, and we will speak them boldly. Sweet friend, we will become not only hearers of the Word but also speakers and doers of the Word (see James 1:22). We will respond to God's calls to action with obedience and great enthusiasm.

But this takes time and discipline. It takes commitment and hard work. It means to always be moving. Our Christian walk should never be stagnant. The crucial question for us is this: Which direction are we moving? Are we moving forward or are we moving backward? Of course, God always wants us to move forward. Hebrews 6:1 exhorts us to "move beyond just the basic teachings . . . [and] push on toward a more perfect understanding."

So let's move forward with Paul to our next "so that."

APPLICATION:

Today, our first "so that" comes from the book of Colossians.

Read Colossians 2:4.

> I tell you this *so that* no one may deceive you by fine-sounding arguments. (NIV; emphasis added)

Read Colossians 2:1–8. Paul speaks of proclaiming Jesus. What did Paul tell the Colossians?

🖋 Why did he tell them this?

We must continually move forward in our faith because when we stand still or slide backward, we open ourselves up to the devil's schemes. Jesus identified Satan in John 8:44 as the "father of lies." Peter warned in 1 Peter 5:8,

> "Be disciplined and stay on guard. Your enemy the devil is prowling around outside like a roaring lion, just waiting *and hoping for the chance* to devour someone."

Let me share a story that brought this verse alive for me.

My son, Bo, and I enjoyed watching Animal Planet when he was young. One evening we watched a fascinating special on lions. The words from 1 Peter came alive as we watched a lioness hunt her prey. After roaming for a time, she came upon a herd of antelope. For hours she lay in wait, pacing back and forth, patiently waiting for the opportune time to attack. Finally, it happened when one member of the herd wandered off alone. The lioness followed at a safe distance. She continued to watch to ensure no other antelope followed. When she felt confident, she made her move. The lioness suddenly appeared before the antelope and circled. We watched as fear mounted in the antelope's body. It was trapped. Alone. Helpless and frantic, it took a step to run.

We must continually move forward in our faith because when we stand still or slide backward, we open ourselves up to the devil's schemes.

> Paul knew the one and only way to overcome Satan was through God's Word and prayer.

In that moment, the lioness lunged with full force, knocking the desperate animal to the ground. The antelope struggled and fought, but eventually fell victim to its predator.

Be warned, my friend: this is a perfect picture of Satan. He stalks God's people. He prowls around looking for our vulnerabilities. He patiently watches and waits until we are alone. And in our moment of weakness, he pounces. His goal: to destroy our faith . . . to tear it to shreds.

The word Paul uses in Colossians 2:4 is "deceive"; the King James Version says "beguile." We are not to be "deceived" by fine-sounding arguments. This is a translation of the Greek word *paralogizomai,* which means "to deceive by false reasoning." It is clear from much of Paul's writing that he engaged in continual spiritual battles with Satan for the hearts of God's people. Satan incessantly attacked, deceiving God's people and trying to lead them astray. Paul relentlessly battled back, teaching God's people the absolute necessity of the Word and prayer.

Paul knew the one and only way to overcome Satan was through God's Word and prayer. Paul directly addressed this in his letter to the Ephesians.

Read Ephesians 6:10–18. What does Paul tell us to do in verses 10–13?

List the six pieces of God's armor in verses 13–17 in the New International Version. Practically, how are we to use each piece?

1.

2.

3.

4.

5.

6.

🖋 Finally, what are we called to do in verse 18?

Paul was especially burdened by the influence of the Gnostics, a group whose beliefs contradicted the very core of Christianity. They rejected God as the Creator of the universe and challenged the truth that Jesus is the center of the Christian faith. They taught that salvation comes by special knowledge, not by Jesus. They rejected equality in the church body and instead advocated a hierarchy. Those with special "hidden knowledge" sat at the top. Everything about the Gnostics' message contradicted the gospel message. Paul wrestled continuously with this group and sought to refute their teachings and expose them as false teachers.

Friend, we engage in this same spiritual battle today. The world bombards us at every turn with worldly temptations. We see them on billboards and television. We hear them on the radio. They become part of our everyday lives in movies, music, books, and magazines. Sometimes they are blatant and sometimes they are cleverly disguised. Because of our fallen nature, we are vulnerable, and if we don't know truth, we will be led astray. If we are not continually in the Word and daily in prayer, we will fall prey to the lies of the world, slip backward, and fall into Satan's trap.

🖋 Let's revisit Colossians 2. What is Paul's purpose in verse 2?

🖋 In Christ, we have what according to Colossians 2:2–3?

What a gift we have in Jesus! Paul teaches that in Him we have "all the treasures of wisdom and knowledge." Any man-made philosophy that contradicts or comes against the wisdom found in God's Word has no place in the life of a believer. We should reject it outright. But how do we identify false teaching?

Listen to these words of Bill Elliff, pastor of the Summit Church in Little Rock, Arkansas:

> [The Devil] has successfully taught us that lying will produce some benefit . . . We will be more respected, more appreciated, live more comfortable if we will just cover the truth. At all costs, we must never admit who we really are. (Think of how it would ruin our reputation!)[7]

When Lauren was in elementary school, she brought home a book that contained content unsuitable for elementary-age children. It was a book more appropriate for middle or even high school students. When I asked the librarian why it was in our library, she provided no explanation. I asked for it to be removed. She said that she would not. In fact, she had no problem with the book and suggested that I simply forbid my daughter from checking it out and reading it.

It became clear that if I wanted it removed, I would have to go over her head. That choice was hard for me, as I liked her very much. I often volunteered in the library, and I feared my actions might affect our relationship. Plus, I knew any action to proceed on my part would require a great investment of my time and energy. I would have to put myself out there not only in our school but also with higher-level administrators in the school system.

The question I had to ask myself was, how would my actions affect Lauren's reputation and mine? Was it worth it for one book that I could just forbid my daughter from reading?

I knew my life would be easier and much more comfortable if I just dropped it.

I prayed and sensed the Lord wanted me to proceed. The world does not make it easy to stand up for Christian values! I followed the instructions given to make this type of request. I read the entire book, noting every page on which I found inappropriate content, and why I felt it was unsuitable. It took hours and hours to document. Then I sent it to the appropriate people.

It took weeks to hear back. When I did, it required more paperwork and conversations. But in the end, praise God, my efforts prevailed. They removed the book from the library!

Was it worth it? Yes. But had I listened to the world and my flesh, I would not have taken on the challenge. The world told me to just keep my problem to myself and take care of it within my family. But my heart and my faith led me otherwise *so that* I could protect all children in Lauren's school from this inappropriate content.

Do you see how being in God's Word changes us from the inside out and leads to "so that" living?

In Colossians 2:4, Paul warns that we must be able to recognize the world's "fine-sounding arguments" (NIV), or "enticing words" (KJV). These words could also be translated "persuasive words." These are words that use logical but false arguments. God calls us to be alert and aware of such words. But that does not just happen.

> The world does not make it easy to stand up for Christian values!

We must first know God's truth to recognize the lies.

We must prepare to be aware. Let me say that again: we must prepare to be aware.

How can we prepare? Be in the Word first and foremost. And as you read and study, pray for discernment. Pray for understanding. Pray for wisdom.

Friend, the church at Colosse had Paul. We have someone even greater. We have Jesus! He is alive in us through God's Holy Spirit. We are rich in the One who is our All in all.

He is our Sufficiency.

He is our Portion.

He is Wisdom.

He is Truth.

He is enough.

He is all we need!

>>> CONCLUDING THOUGHTS:

My research revealed a wonderful quote in a sermon preached by Thomas Bevers. I'm not sure if he is the author, but I thought it a fitting conclusion for this chapter:

The Bible

This Book is the mind of God, the state of man, the way of salvation, the doom of sinners, and the happiness of believers. Its doctrines are holy, its precepts are binding; its histories are true, and its decisions are immutable. Read it to be wise, believe it to be safe, practice it to be holy. It contains light to direct you, food to support you, and comfort to cheer you. It is the traveler's map, the pilgrim's staff, the pilot's compass, the soldier's sword, and the Christian's character. Here paradise is restored, heaven opened, and the gates of hell disclosed. Christ is its grand subject, our good its design, and the glory of God its end. It should fill the memory, rule the heart, and guide the feet. Read it slowly, frequently, prayerfully. It is a mine of wealth, a paradise of glory, and a river of pleasure. Follow its precepts and it will lead you to Calvary, to the empty tomb, to a resurrected life in Christ; yes, to glory itself, for eternity.[8]

How we have delighted in the Lord's Word in this chapter! I don't know about you, but my heart is overflowing with *truth*!

What I have learned is that I must fill my mind with God's spoken Word. Here are two important principles to remember:

1. You and I act on what we *believe* and not on what we *know*.

2. What fills our hearts and minds will determine our choices.

Based on how God has spoken to your heart, complete the thought below.

God spoke so that . . .

MY CALL TO ACTION:

Prayerfully ask the Lord if He has a call to action for you based on our lesson. If you hear "Yes," write a prayer below asking the Lord to help you obey what you have heard. List a few steps you will take to carry out your call to action.

CHAPTER THREE

Pray So That...

MEMORY VERSE: LET US THEN APPROACH THE THRONE OF GRACE WITH CONFIDENCE, **SO THAT** WE MAY RECEIVE MERCY AND FIND GRACE TO HELP US IN OUR TIME OF NEED.

—Hebrews 4:16 (NIV; emphasis added)

PRAYER:

Heavenly Father, thank You for the gift of prayer. I invite You to speak a fresh Word to me this week. I don't want my prayer time to be a religious ritual that I do each day. I don't want it to be another thing I check off my "to do" list. Teach me to pray with power. I want my prayers to be effective and bring results that will glorify and honor You and You alone. Feed me Your living and active Word. Plant it deep in my heart so that I can recall it and pray it with my lips. As I speak Your Word and hold it before You, I trust You to honor it . . . for it is Your Word. Thank You that Your Word, when prayed, will not return void but will accomplish what You desire and achieve the purposes for which You sent it. Thank You that it will prosper in everything for which it is sent! Give me the courage to come boldly before Your throne of grace. When I arrive, Father, meet me there. Shower me with the presence of Your Holy Spirit. Make Yourself known to me. Be at work in my prayers. Show me Your glory, Lord! Show me Your glory! I love You so much. I ask all this in the name of Your Son, Jesus. Amen.

PART ONE:
Pray Continually

Do you long to go deeper with God in prayer?

Today we begin a beautiful journey, and my heart's desire for each of us is that through this chapter, God will meet us where we are and take us to deeper places with Him in prayer.

Sylvia Gunter, author of *Prayer Portions*, defines prayer this way: "Prayer is radically and gloriously encountering God, knowing Him better and loving Him more."[1]

It's not about a list. There is no agenda. There is no formula. Prayer is simply a glorious encounter with the One who created us. Listen to these words from Zephaniah 3:17:

> For the LORD your God is living among you. He is a mighty savior. He will take delight in you with gladness. With his love, he will calm all your fears. He will rejoice over you with joyful songs. (NLT)

Can you imagine anything more wonderful? Our God delights in us, calms us, and rejoices over us. He is intimately involved with us.

🖋 Share a bit about your prayer life, if any, growing up.

🖋 Do you pray now? If so, describe your prayer life (time of day, frequency, manner of prayer—written or oral).

🖋 If you pray, why do you pray?

⇒⟫ APPLICATION:

Before Jesus came to earth, prayer looked very different. God's people did not have the same access to God that we have today. They had to go through a priest. Let's go back to the time of Moses to learn a bit more.

After God delivered His people from Egypt, He instructed the Israelites, through Moses, to build Him a sanctuary so that He could dwell among them (Exodus 25:8–9). At God's direction, Moses and the Israelites built the first tabernacle. Within the tabernacle, Moses built two rooms separated by a heavy veil, as directed by God. The room behind the veil was called the Holy of Holies and contained the ark of the covenant. God's very presence resided in this holy room, hovering over the ark of the covenant. Jewish law allowed one priest access to this room one time a year. That one day, that one man had the privilege of coming into the presence of God to pray, offer a blood sacrifice, and ask forgiveness for his sin as well as the sins of the Israelites (Exodus 25–26). The sacrifice had to be a perfect, unblemished male animal (Leviticus 1).

Without the priest and the sacrifice, the people had no access. Sin stood in the way and had stood in the way since God created the first man.

But God had a plan.

In part one of God's plan, He created man (and woman) to be in perfect fellowship with Him. He created them to rule over His creation. But because of their selfish choices to eat from the forbidden Tree of Knowledge of Good and Evil in the garden of Eden, they lost that perfect fellowship. They chose to believe and follow the lies of Satan rather than the truth of God.

God responded to their sin by banishing them from His presence. He removed them from the garden forever, placing cherubim and a flaming sword flashing back and forth to guard the way to the Tree of Life (Genesis 1–3).

Why? Because our God is holy, and His holiness prevents Him from being in the presence of sin. When Adam and Eve disobeyed God's Word, they sinned and lost fellowship with Him. That sin has been downloaded to every generation of people since that time, including ours.

And even though the Israelites were God's chosen people, because of sin, not even they had direct access to God.

To remedy this problem, God set in motion the next stage of His plan . . . salvation through His one and only Son. Salvation would bring God's people back into perfect fellowship with Him.

> Adam and Eve chose to believe and follow the lies of Satan rather than the truth of God.

To accomplish this, God sent His Son, Jesus, to be the last and final blood sacrifice. Jesus was the ultimate, perfect sacrifice. A high priest would no longer be needed as an intermediary between God and His people.

Friend, what this means for you and me is that we, unlike the Israelites, now have direct access to God. We have the opportunity to enter into God's presence through prayer anytime, anywhere. Hebrews 10:19–22 explains:

> So, my friends, Jesus by His blood gives us courage to enter the most holy place. He has created for us a new and living way through the curtain, that is, through His flesh. Since we have a great High Priest who presides over the house of God, let us draw near with true hearts full of faith, with hearts rinsed clean of any evil conscience, and with bodies cleansed with pure water.

Matthew 27:51 tells us that at the very moment Jesus cried out and gave up His spirit "the temple curtain was torn in half, from top to bottom."

God, through the death of His Son, opened the way for you and me to enter into His presence!

Now that we have that access, what exactly are we supposed to do with it? We are to pray!

So what is prayer?

Prayer is a gift.

Prayer is a privilege.

Prayer is *two-way* communication with God.

Prayer is a love relationship with the God who created us.

Because of Jesus' sacrifice, we can "approach [God's] throne of grace with confidence" (Hebrews 4:16 NIV).

When you sit before the Lord in prayer, do you approach Him confidently? If you answered no, share why you find it hard to pray with confidence.

Friend, Jesus gave up His life so that you could be in relationship with Him . . . so that you could enter into His presence and have fellowship with Him. If you feel uncomfortable praying or feel unworthy to pray, spend time thanking Jesus for what He has done and ask Him to make His sacrifice a reality in your life. *Believe* He did this just for you . . . because He did. He longs for you to come to Him in prayer. Remember, He gave up His life to make it happen. He desires to hear your praises, your hopes, your dreams, and every cry of your heart.

Pray with me . . .

Sweet Jesus, thank You for dying on the cross at Calvary, for tearing the curtain in two and making a way for me to be united as one with You. Help me to fully accept this gift. Open my heart to know You more intimately and to know how much You value me and find me worthy of Your love and Your time. Fill my heart with prayers of praise and thanksgiving and teach me to pray powerfully and effectively to make a difference in my life and the life of Your kingdom.

Let's look at what Jesus says about prayer. Jesus shares a specific teaching on prayer in Luke 11:1–13. This is where we find the cherished Lord's Prayer. Did you memorize this prayer when you were a child? I remember it being one of the first prayers I learned.

> Jesus desires to hear your praises, your hopes, your dreams, and every cry of your heart.

Jesus had taken His disciples to a place to pray, and when He had finished praying, His disciples asked Him to teach them to pray. Take a few minutes to read the Lord's Prayer.

Read Luke 11:1–4.

Since most of us are probably familiar with the Lord's Prayer, we will focus not on the prayer itself, but on the verses following the prayer.

Read Luke 11:5–13.

What do you learn in verses 5–8?

What do you learn in verses 9–10?

What do you learn in verses 11–13?

In this passage, Jesus urges boldness and persistence in prayer. He also tells His disciples that God is the giver of good gifts, and He will generously give those gifts, especially the gift of His Holy Spirit.

Paul, too, speaks of prayer, in Colossians 4:2: "Pray, *and keep praying.* Be alert and thankful when you pray." The NIV says, "Devote yourselves to prayer." The King James Version says, "Continue in prayer." The Greek word translated "continue" means "to be strong towards, to endure in, or persevere in." Another definition reads, "To give constant attention to."

So, the first part of Colossians 4:2 teaches us to "devote ourselves to" or "persevere in" prayer.

Define "persevere."

Practically speaking, what does this look like in a prayer life?

Let's dig a bit more. First Thessalonians 5:17 says, "Pray constantly." The King James Version says to pray "without ceasing." Interestingly, in the Greek this word does not speak of something uninterrupted, but of something constantly recurring. We are called to a continual state of prayer . . . not that we stop and start often, but that we continually keep our hearts in a ready state of prayer.

Paul does not stop after instructing us to pray continually. Why? Because to pray continually, without purpose and/or direction, is not effective prayer. Paul gives more direction: "Be alert and thankful."

To be alert implies activity on our part. The book of Ephesians confirms this: "Pray always. Pray in the Spirit . . . and be on the lookout *until evil has been stayed*" (6:18). These words speak of watching with purpose, being intent upon something. When we pray, God invites us into a two-way relationship that involves two-way communication. We need to eagerly anticipate answers to our prayers. We need to watch for Him to be at work.

One way to "be on the lookout" is to look for answers. Open the Word with great expectancy to hear from the Lord, praying, *Show me, God*. Look for a change in your circumstances, praying, *Show me, God*. Listen for words of wisdom from friends, praying, *Show me, God*. Listen for the whispers of the Holy Spirit, praying, *Show me, God*. By doing this, you are positioning your heart to pray continually.

Share a memorable time in your life when you were watchful and experienced answered prayer.

A dear friend of mine, Lisa Allen, shared a great way to bring watchfulness alive in our prayer lives. She calls them prayer triggers. When you have a person for whom God calls you to pray, be creative. Think of something that reminds you of the person. Invite God to open your eyes to see that trigger and use it to remind you to pray. Lisa loves any and all things leopard, so whenever I see anything leopard, the Lord reminds me to pray for her. If you assign triggers to special people in your life, think of how many times throughout the day you will pray! Again, you are positioning your heart to pray continually.

Our pastor's wife, Marilynn Chadwick, author of *Sometimes He Whispers, Sometimes He Roars: Learning to Hear the Voice of God*, looks for

We need to eagerly anticipate answers to our prayers. We need to watch for God to be at work.

> Whether we are shopping, driving, working, cleaning, or just resting, God wants to be a part.

"watchwords." When she is praying for someone or about something, she looks for a personal word from the Lord that speaks to her prayer. By doing this, she increases her alertness to God's voice.[2]

For example, Marilynn writes that she knew a missionary couple who lived and served in Africa. When her friends faced situations that seemed impossible, they remembered David and his battle against Goliath, and the wife's "watchwords" became "one smooth stone." When she faced a difficult trial, she thought of her "one smooth stone," and it reminded her to trust that God would provide what she needed for victory just as He had provided for David. Watchwords, like prayer triggers, position our hearts to pray continually.

These examples demonstrate that praying without ceasing is not praying twenty-four hours a day, seven days a week, fifty-two weeks a year. Rather, it is an attitude of the heart. Rick Warren writes in *The Purpose Driven Life*, "*Everything* you do can be 'spending time with God' if he is invited to be a part of it and you stay aware of his presence."[3]

God wants to hear from us. Remember Zephaniah 3:17? He delights in us. He rejoices over us. Whatever we are doing or thinking, He seeks to be included. Whether we are shopping, driving, working, cleaning, or just resting, He wants to be a part.

Let's revisit Colossians 4:2.

Paul calls us to devote ourselves to prayer, to being alert, and to

_____ .

🖋 Why does he include being thankful?

🖋 **Read Psalm 103:1–5.** List five reasons the psalmist gives for us to be thankful.

Author and speaker Carole Lewis shares in her book *A Thankful Heart: How Gratitude Brings Hope and Healing to Our Lives*, "When we're thankful, we agree with God. When we're thankful, we praise His name. Being thankful puts sorrow in perspective. It's an antidote to bitterness, anger and despair."[4]

If we limit prayer to asking God to meet our needs and answer our long list of requests, prayer becomes selfish and self-centered. It is no longer the two-way communication God created for us on the cross at Calvary. Thankfulness ensures our hearts focus not only on us but also on God and His goodness.

🖋 Will you take some time to thank God for the simple, everyday things for which you are grateful? Write your prayer of thanksgiving below. I encourage you to do this regularly. No matter what is going on in your life, take a bit of time to tell God everything for which you are thankful.

⟫ CONCLUDING THOUGHTS:

I hope you have learned much about prayer in this section. Prayer is something we must actively do. So, beginning now, I invite you to be active in your prayer life.

Prayerfully choose someone for whom you can pray. Choose a prayer trigger that will remind you to pray for that person. Record below or in your journal how God works as you faithfully pray using your prayer trigger.

Based on how God has spoken to your heart, complete the thought below.

Pray so that . . .

PART TWO:
Watch and Pray

MEMORY VERSE: LET US THEN APPROACH THE THRONE OF
GRACE WITH CONFIDENCE, **SO THAT** WE MAY RECEIVE MERCY
AND FIND GRACE TO HELP US IN OUR TIME OF NEED.

–Hebrews 4:16 (NIV; emphasis added)

Open your Bible to Matthew 26. After finishing His teaching in the Upper Room, Jesus led His disciples on a walk that ended at the entrance of the Garden of Gethsemane. Upon arrival, Jesus asked eight of the disciples to stay behind, and took Peter, James, and John with Him. This was the third time in His ministry that He had intentionally chosen these three disciples to accompany Him on a momentous occasion (the other two times are found in Matthew 17:1, during the Transfiguration; and in Mark 5:37, during the healing of Jairus's daughter).

Scripture tells us that Jesus grew sorrowful and deeply distressed because He knew what lay ahead on Calvary. He wanted and needed His friends close by for prayer and encouragement. How precious it is to witness Jesus pouring out His heart, revealing the reality of His humanity:

> "My soul is overwhelmed with grief, to the point of death. Stay here and keep watch with Me." (Matthew 26:38)

Friend, let these words soak in. They show us the part of Jesus that was taken from among men. He was one of us and, therefore, experienced our every emotion. He felt pain. He felt sorrow. He felt loneliness. He felt despair.

His time had come. Death was imminent. He coveted the comfort and nearness of His closest friends.

🖋 Why was Jesus overwhelmed with grief?

It's strange to think of Jesus being overwhelmed with grief when He knew with certainty He would be raised from the dead and reunited with His Father in heaven. But His sorrow was for what was about to happen to Him physically and spiritually. He knew in the depths of His soul the extreme pain and agony the next hours and days would bring. He would be humiliated, persecuted, tortured, and abused. Jesus would endure more pain and suffering than any one man should ever have to endure. Jesus' obedience to His Father's will meant that He would be separated from His Father for the first time ever.

Jesus was about to drink the "cup" (John 18:11) that His Father had prepared for Him, a cup that required that Jesus bear in His own body the sins of the world.

🖋 Why did God ordain this moment in time for His one and only Son? (2 Corinthians 5:21; Galatians 3:13–14)

And, friend, we must never forget that Jesus acted *willingly*. Yes, He wrestled with God. But His wrestling was not about obedience. He was ready and willing to obey. His wrestling was really about processing His human emotions and the suffering He was about to endure. What a gift it is for us to witness Jesus' humanity and deity collide in the shadows of the Garden. Because we are given this glimpse of Jesus, we can *know* that He truly can identify with us in our pain and suffering.

APPLICATION:

Now let's leave Jesus' wrestling with God and return to His interaction with Peter, James, and John in Matthew 26:40–41:

> So you couldn't keep watch with Me for just one short hour? . . . The spirit is willing, but the body is weak. Watch and pray and take care **[so] that** you are not pulled down during a time of testing. (Bold emphasis added)

What happened when Jesus asked His disciples to "watch and pray"?

Though Jesus' friends knew the agony and sorrow Jesus was experiencing, they could not stay awake to watch and pray. They slept. Not once, not twice, but three times, Jesus asked them to pray. And each time He returned from praying, He found them asleep.

After the first time, Jesus gave them the gentle reproof and warning found in Matthew 26:41. Notice, we see the word "watch" again. Jesus says, "**Watch** and pray and take care **[so] that** you are not pulled down during a time of testing" (bold emphasis added).

What do you think Jesus' tone was as He spoke the words, "So you couldn't keep watch with Me for just one short hour?"

🖋 Who does He address specifically? Why do you suppose Jesus singles him out? (See Matthew 26:31–35.)

I wonder if Jesus had hoped for more from His friends. He had only asked for one hour, just one hour. They could not give it. Perhaps if they had truly understood all that He had told them about what was to happen, about what He was to suffer, things might have been different. Maybe they would have sacrificed that single hour of sleep. We will never know.

🖋 What about you? Is Your Savior asking of you something you are not giving? Take some time to listen and pray before you answer. Share what you hear and feel below.

Jesus tells the disciples exactly why He wants them to "watch and pray" in Matthew 26:41.

🖋 What is the "so that" here?

❧ What is the time of testing of which He speaks here?

"Temptation" as used here is a translation of the Greek word *peirasmos*, which usually refers to "trials with a beneficial purpose and effect." They are divinely permitted trials and temptations. As specifically used here, it refers to trials and temptations entered into by a person's disobedience or carelessness. Matthew Henry, in his commentary, wrote, "There was an hour of temptation drawing on, and very near; the troubles of Christ were temptations to his followers to disbelieve and distrust him, to deny and desert him, and renounce all relation to him. There was danger of their entering into the temptation, as into a snare or trap; of their entering into a parley with it, or a good opinion of it, of their being influenced by it, and inclining to comply with it; which is the first step toward being overcome by it."[5]

Jesus knew the danger and trouble that lay ahead for His disciples. Spending time praying with and for Jesus would have not only blessed them but also equipped and empowered them for what they were about to endure.

The same is true for us, sweet friend. Our God is all-knowing. He alone knows what our future holds. God gave the gift of prayer, in part, to prepare us for that future. It is in and through our prayer time that God girds us up for the trials, battles, and temptations that will come our way. Some of the trials may be self-induced, that is, brought on by our own actions. Others may be sent by God to rebuke and discipline us and draw us back to obedience. This may sound harsh, but it's no different from the way earthly parents discipline their children to bring them back into obedience. Just as parents want what is best for their children, God both wants and knows what is best for us.

Rick Warren once said, "God is more interested in your character than your comfort. God is more interested in making your life holy than He is in making your life happy."[6]

What are Jesus' last words in Matthew 26:41? Explain what He means.

Jesus was so gentle in His rebuke. Did you notice? He only rebuked the disciples once, after the first time He found them sleeping. The second time, He let them sleep. The third time, He told them to get up, for the time had come for His betrayal. Jesus had compassion. Because He, too, was human, He knew they were physically, mentally, and emotionally weak.

Friend, our flesh is weak. It will always seek to meet its own needs. David recognized this in Psalm 51:10–12. He wrote this psalm after the prophet Nathan had chastised him for committing adultery with Bathsheba. David prayed, "Renew a steadfast spirit within me" and "restore to me the joy of your salvation and grant me a willing spirit, to sustain me" (NIV).

Paul recognized this same fleshly struggle in Romans 7:15–25.

Read Romans 7:15–25 and explain in your own words the struggle of which Paul is speaking.

When Paul says "I," he is referring to the flesh (our old nature). Our flesh provides that beachhead, spoken of in our earlier lesson, for sin to operate in our lives. Paul wanted to make good choices just as you and I want to make good choices. We don't want to have an anxiety attack when our boss adds one more "to do" to our already lengthy "to do" lists. We don't want to lose it when our husband forgets something on the grocery list. We don't want to yell at our children when they talk back. We don't want to speak unkind words and make rude gestures to the person who cut us off on the freeway. But we do.

We have two options. The first tugs at us to choose God's way and glorify God. The other pulls at us to choose our way and satisfy self. We will choose one or the other. The only way to escape the pull of the flesh is to strengthen the Spirit. We must choose to feed the flesh or feed the Spirit. Feeding the Spirit requires that we be in the Word and that we pray. The more we engage in these spiritual disciplines, the more the Spirit will win out over the flesh, and the more Christ will be glorified in and through our actions and our speech.

> *The only way to escape the pull of the flesh is to strengthen the Spirit.*

IF YOU WANT TO GO DEEPER:

Read Galatians 2:20–21 and share how Paul's words here relate to what he speaks of in the Romans passage.

🖋 **Read Galatians 5:16–17.** Rewrite these verses in your own words.

🖋 Do you have an area or areas in your life where you specifically struggle with giving in to the flesh? If you answered yes, share what it is.

🖋 Does "the world" contribute to your struggle in any way? If yes, explain how.

🖋 Share some steps you can take to combat the flesh and feed the Spirit to gain victory in this area.

⇒〉CONCLUDING THOUGHTS:

The good news, my friend, is that as believers in Jesus, we have complete and total victory over our flesh. Because of Jesus' death and resurrection, the indwelling presence of the Holy Spirit in us has the power to overcome sin every time! Will you celebrate this truth with me?

What a gift we have in Jesus!

Yes, we will engage in battles, some self-induced and some allowed by the hand of our sovereign God. Yes, we will struggle with making more faith-filled, rather than faith-less, choices. The question for us to ask is, are we prepared? Have we done our part to come out victorious on the other side?

Prayer is a vital prerequisite to this victory. We must seek to be in constant communion with God. We must set our hearts and minds on the things of God. When we do, we stand on a firm foundation. So, even if our flesh fails temporarily and we falter or disobey, our inner man remains steadfast. God will soften our hearts, convict our spirits, and enable us to make more faith-filled choices in the midst of our messy lives.

Based on how God has spoken to your heart, complete the thought below.

Pray so that . . .

PART THREE:
Riches in Christ

MEMORY VERSE: LET US THEN APPROACH THE THRONE OF GRACE WITH CONFIDENCE, **SO THAT** WE MAY RECEIVE MERCY AND FIND GRACE TO HELP US IN OUR TIME OF NEED.

–Hebrews 4:16 (NIV; emphasis added)

As you work on your memory verse this week, please know I have prayed for you. If you are struggling, remember the power of the Holy Spirit lives within you to equip and empower you to memorize God's Word and tuck it deep into your heart.

Remember Sylvia Gunter's definition of prayer? She said, "Prayer is radically and gloriously encountering God, knowing Him better and loving Him more."[7] Until I studied prayer in depth, I never thought of prayer as an avenue to know God. It was more like a task. I would praise God for His goodness, thank Him for answered prayer, and tell Him my needs. I would pray step-by-step, using a checklist, because that is who I am . . . a list girl. Give me a list at the beginning of the day, and I will knock it out by the end. That is a gold star day for me!

But a few years ago, when I wrote a study on the book of Ephesians, Paul taught me much about prayer that I did not know. Today we will study a passage from one of Paul's most beautiful prayers.

Before we examine his prayer, let's begin with a bit of background on Ephesians. Paul's purpose in writing the letter was to draw the Ephesian church back into a relationship with Jesus. He saw a church that had done great works but had fallen out of love with Jesus. He

> *Until I studied prayer in depth, I never thought of prayer as an avenue to know God.*

wrote this letter to encourage them to love God and each other on a deeper level.

Read Ephesians 1:1–14.

Paul spent the first fourteen verses of Ephesians 1 teaching his audience about the spiritual blessings that were theirs in Christ. He told them they were chosen, adopted, redeemed, forgiven, enlightened, sealed with the Holy Spirit, and beneficiaries of a great inheritance.

Following this teaching, Paul prayed for his audience not only to know but also *to understand* the great riches they had in Christ. He wanted them to walk confidently in these riches. This kind of confidence cannot take root when knowledge stays only in the mind. So, what follows Paul's teaching is a passionate prayer in which Paul prays for God to move the Ephesian church from head knowledge to heart knowledge.

Read Ephesians 1:15–23.

Although Paul prayed this prayer for the Ephesian church, it's written for us today as well. Romans 15:4 says:

> For everything that was written in the past was written to teach us, *so that* through endurance and the encouragement of the Scriptures we might have hope. (NIV; emphasis added)

I pray Paul's prayer for each one of us, that as we learn and study God's Word, He will move it from our heads to our hearts. Friend, I want you to know and believe that the more you expose your heart to God's Word, the more it will consume your heart and transform your mind (Romans 12:2).

APPLICATION:

Let's open our Bibles to Ephesians 1:15, where Paul begins his prayer. He leads off with "This is why"; other translations say "Therefore."

Anytime we see these words in Scripture, they indicate that the author wants the reader to examine the preceding verses. Paul had just taken his audience on a beautiful journey through the riches they had in Christ. He knew that many in the church understood what he had said intellectually. But intellectual understanding was not enough. He wanted it to seep deep into their hearts because he knew that truth must reach a person's heart for life change to happen. Paul ached for life change in this church.

Reread Ephesians 1:17:

> God of our Lord Jesus the Anointed, Father of Glory: *I call out to You on behalf of Your people.* Give them minds ready to receive wisdom and revelation **so [that]** they will truly know You. (Bold emphasis added)

For what does Paul pray in Ephesians 1:17?

What is the "so that" in his prayer?

The key words in this verse are "wisdom" and "revelation." Remember, God, through His Holy Spirit, deposited the words of Scripture into the hearts and minds of its authors. They, in turn, recorded those words. God then graciously gave us the gift of His Holy Spirit to enable us to understand those words and make them relevant to our lives.

The rub here is what we do with the written Word. The choice is ours. We can read it every day with a hunger and thirst to learn, or we can read it when it's convenient and suits our needs and schedule. We will not gain deep understanding of the Word when our only interaction with it is through worship on Sunday or a devotional each day. Not that there isn't value in each of these. There is. They may minister to us in the moment. They may teach us a truth. But it is not the kind of interaction that will bring life change.

Paul prays for the church to have "wisdom and revelation." Revelation is the unveiling of a spiritual truth (or truths). Wisdom gives insight and understanding into those spiritual truths. Without "wisdom and revelation" *from the Holy Spirit*, it is impossible to understand the things of God.

Read Isaiah 11:2; John 14:15–16; and John 16:12–14. What do these passages teach you about the role of the Holy Spirit?

Do you see that God sent His Holy Spirit for the very purpose of teaching us the secrets of the kingdom of God? Early on, that was Jesus' role. After Jesus' resurrection and ascension, it became the Holy Spirit's role. This is why Scripture seems like foolishness to unbelievers. First Corinthians 1:18 says:

> For people who are stumbling toward ruin, the message of the cross is nothing but a tall tale for fools by a fool. But for those of us who are already experiencing the reality of being rescued *and made right*, it is nothing short of God's power.

The Holy Spirit's role is essential in the growth of a believer. The Holy Spirit reveals truth to us from the Word, and then gives us the wisdom to understand and apply it. It is the Holy Spirit who brings the living and active Word alive and makes it relevant.

God sent His Holy Spirit to indwell us *so that* we may "know" Him better. The "knowledge" Paul speaks of is a translation of the Greek word *epignosis* and refers not only to abstract knowledge or objective facts about God, but also knowing Him intimately . . . knowing His heart, His character, and His will. Never forget that we are made in the image of God. So the more intimately you and I know our Father in heaven, the better we will know and understand ourselves and how God wants us to live and move and *exist* while on this earth (see Acts 17:26–28).

Let's examine our next verse from the Ephesians 1 passage:

> I pray also that the eyes of your heart may be enlightened *in order that* you may know the hope to which he has called you, the riches of his glorious inheritance in the saints. (v. 18 NIV; emphasis added)

For what does Paul pray in Ephesians 1:18?

What is the "so that" (read, "in order that") in his prayer?

Paul prays that the "eyes of your heart may be enlightened." Most believe this a continuation of verse 17, thereby expanding on the riches that are ours in Christ.

Read 1 Corinthians 2:9–12. Share how this passage confirms what we are learning in Ephesians.

As unbelievers, we lived in darkness. Christ called us out of darkness into His marvelous light (1 Peter 2:9). Paul now prays for that light to shine into our hearts. He is not referring to a literal beating heart. Rather, he speaks here of our inner man . . . the saved part of us . . . our minds, our emotions, and our wills. It's the part of us that sees, hears, and experiences the things of God. Those without Christ can neither see nor hear nor experience God. Jesus said these very words in Matthew 13:13:

> "This is why I speak to them in parables: 'Though seeing, they do not see; though hearing, they do not hear or understand.'" (NIV)

The inability to see and understand spiritual things is not a matter of intelligence. It's a matter of the heart. Without the Holy Spirit, our hearts remain in darkness.

Paul prays for enlightenment so that we may know the hope to which we are called. Our hope, of course, is God's promise of that glorious day when Jesus will return for His bride, the church. God did not save us to sit and soak in all that He teaches. He saved us to live lives worthy of the hope He has given. He saved us so that we can make a difference in His world!

Our challenge is to live out our hope in a way that draws others to the hope we have found. What is so wonderful is that along the way, we receive God's riches and blessings. Although they are too numerous to count, I want to share a few:

We are the apple of His eye. (Zechariah 2:8)

Our names are engraved on the palms of His hands. (Isaiah 49:16)

He takes pleasure in us. (Psalm 149:4)

We cannot comprehend all that He has prepared for those who love Him. (1 Corinthians 2:9)

The things He does for us are immeasurably greater than we could ever ask or imagine. (Ephesians 3:20)

Share a few of your favorite "riches" in Christ.

Friend, it's impossible to take in these truths all at once. They are too magnificent to comprehend in one or even a few sittings with our Bible. They take a lifetime of learning. As we faithfully seek God in His Word, He will begin revealing them one by one, bringing them alive, and enabling us to appropriate them.

Dr. David Jeremiah shares a great story that is relevant to our lesson today. He speaks of a sheep rancher named Ira Yates who lived during the Great Depression. Like many Americans during this time, Mr. Yates struggled to make a living.

One day, a geological survey team from a large oil company asked for permission to drill on his property at no cost to him. He agreed.

After drilling 250 feet, they found nothing. Same result at 500 feet and 1,000 feet. But at 1,100 feet they hit one of the largest oil reservoirs ever discovered in America. They pumped 80,000 barrels of oil a day, and Mr. Yates became a millionaire overnight![8] He was a real-life Jed Clampett (the hillbilly-turned-millionaire in *The Beverly Hillbillies*).

Why do I tell you this story? What in the world does it have to do with what we are studying? Before the oil company discovered oil on Mr. Yates's property, did he have the rights to all that oil? Yes, he absolutely did. His problem was twofold. First, he had no knowledge there was oil underneath his land. And second, when he gained the knowledge, he had no resources to access what was rightfully his.

Sadly, many of us live exactly like Mr. Yates. We invite Jesus into our hearts. We receive the gift of His Holy Spirit. But we are ignorant of the riches that accompany that gift. Either we don't know what we have in Christ, or we are aware but don't know how to access it.

You and I have the knowledge. Our next step is to dig deep into our reservoir of riches. So let's take the next step . . . pray and mine the wonderful riches of wisdom and knowledge available to us in Christ.

IF YOU WANT TO GO DEEPER:

Paul's prayer ends with verses 19–23.

Read Ephesians 1:19–23. For what does Paul pray in verse 19?

Who is the source of that power?

🖋 How does Paul describe that power?

🖋 What does Paul want God to do with that power?

I want you to grasp the enormity of the power that resides within every believer. It's the power that parted the Red Sea. It's the power that raised Lazarus from the dead. It's the power that raised Jesus from the grave. It's the power that took Jesus up to the heavens and seated Him at the right hand of God, and that exalted Christ far "above all rule, authority, power, and dominion; over every name invoked, *over every title bestowed* in this age and the next" (Ephesians 1:21; see also Philippians 2:9–11).

And through this power, God "has placed all things beneath His feet and anointed Him as the head over all things for His church. This church is His body, the fullness of the One who fills all in all" (Ephesians 1:22–23). Jesus is *all* authority by virtue of His position. Jesus rules over everything that was, is, and is to come.

This power, sweet friend, *this power* lives inside of you! This power is available to you and me 24/7.

No sin we have committed is beyond His forgiveness. No choice we have made is beyond His redeeming. No sickness we have is beyond His healing. No mountain in our way is beyond His moving.

Invite Christ to manifest this power afresh in your life today!

CONCLUDING THOUGHTS:

When we walk in intimate fellowship with our heavenly Father, He empowers us to live in the fullness of His wisdom, knowledge, riches, and power. This kind of relationship does not just happen. Many obstacles will cross our paths to thwart God's highest and best for us. Paul saw that in the Ephesian church, and we see it in our own lives. That is why Paul prayed fervently for them. And it is why we need to pray fervently for ourselves and one another. Without the foundation of the Word and prayer pouring into our lives, we will never live in the abundant riches God has to offer.

Once again, based on how God has spoken to your heart, complete the thought below.

Pray so that . . .

PART FOUR:
»»» Help Me with My Unbelief

MEMORY VERSE: LET US THEN APPROACH THE THRONE OF
GRACE WITH CONFIDENCE, **SO THAT** WE MAY RECEIVE MERCY
AND FIND GRACE TO HELP US IN OUR TIME OF NEED.

—Hebrews 4:16 (NIV; emphasis added)

"I believe, Lord. Help me to believe!" (Mark 9:24). Do you feel this
way sometimes? You pray and want to believe that God will answer
your prayers. You know that His Word says in Christ all things are
possible (Philippians 4:13). But your circumstances do not change.
Your answer doesn't come.

The opening sentence of our lesson comes from a story in Mark
9 that speaks directly to this question.

Read Mark 9:14–29.

Jesus led Peter, James, and John up the Mount of Transfiguration,
where Jesus was transfigured before their very eyes (Mark 9:2–8). As
they descended the mountain, they saw a large crowd gathered. In
the middle of the crowd, they saw the disciples arguing with the
teachers of the law.

Right when the crowd saw Jesus, they were overcome with awe
and surged forward immediately, *nearly running over the disciples*.

JESUS *(to the scribes)*: What are you debating with My disciples?
What would you like to know?

FATHER *(in the crowd)*: Teacher, I have brought my son to You. He
is filled with an unclean spirit. He cannot speak, and when the
spirit takes control of him, he is thrown to the ground *to wail
and moan*, to foam at the mouth, to grind his teeth, and to stiffen

up. I brought him to Your followers, but they could do nothing with him. *Can You help us?*

JESUS: O faithless generation, how long must I be among you? How long do I have to put up with you? Bring the boy to Me.

They brought the boy toward Jesus; but as soon as He drew near; the spirit took control of the boy and threw him on the ground, where he rolled, foaming at the mouth.

JESUS *(to the father)*: How long has he been like this?

FATHER: Since he was a baby. This spirit has thrown him often into the fire and sometimes into the water, trying to destroy him. *I have run out of options; I have tried everything.* But if there's anything You can do, please, have pity on us and help us.

JESUS: *What do you mean,* "If there's anything?" All things are possible, if you only believe.

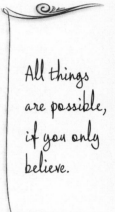

All things are possible, if you only believe.

FATHER *(crying in desperation)*: I believe, Lord. Help me to believe!

Jesus noticed that a crowd had gathered around them now. He issued a command to the unclean spirit.

JESUS: Listen up, you no-talking, no-hearing demon. I Myself am ordering you to come out of him now. Come out, and don't ever come back!

The spirit shrieked and caused the boy to thrash about; then it came out of the boy and left him lying as still as death. Many of those in the crowd whispered that he was dead. But Jesus took the boy by the hand and lifted him to his feet. (Mark 9:15–27)

🖋 What word does Jesus use to describe the generation? To whom is He referring?

Jesus' words expressed His exasperation with the sin of unbelief. We will dive into this in our application section. But before we move on, it's vital you know that, in Luke 9:1, Jesus gave the disciples the "power and authority to free people from all demonic spirits and to heal them of diseases." So why were they not able to cast the demon out? Did they never actually receive the power? Did Jesus decide they were not worthy of that power and take it back?

The disciples were confused as well. So they asked Jesus why they were unable to drive out the demons. Jesus answered in Mark 9:29, "That sort *of powerful spirit* can only be conquered with much prayer [and fasting]." In Matthew's gospel, He answered, "Because you have so little faith" (17:20).

Do the answers Mark and Matthew gave contradict each other? Absolutely not! Faith and prayer go hand in hand.

🖋 Share from your own experience how faith and prayer go hand in hand.

APPLICATION:

Reread Mark 9:14–19.

Returning to our story, Jesus rebuked the disciples for their failure to exercise the power He had given them in Luke 9:1. His words are strong, "O faithless generation." (Most scholars agree Jesus was referring to His disciples and not to the crowd in general.)

What do you think was going through Jesus' mind as He looked upon His disciples? What was His heart feeling in that moment?

Jesus' words reveal His disappointment and great frustration. Why could the disciples not do what He had commissioned them to do? Perhaps they lacked confidence because Jesus was not with them. Or maybe they felt they needed the presence of Peter, James, and John, their leaders. Or perhaps the crowd intimidated them. Maybe the crowd was mocking them. We don't know.

But the disciples were not the only ones who lacked faith in this story.

Who else lacked faith? (v. 22)

🖋 Explain his interaction with Jesus, focusing on his words in Mark 9:21–22.

Jesus asked the father how long his son had been sick. The father answered, "Since he was a baby." Can you imagine the fear with which this father lived . . . never knowing what this spirit would do to his son? Can't you hear the desperation in his words? "But if there's **anything** you can do, please, have pity on us and help us" (Mark 9:22; bold emphasis added).

The father began with the word "But." This word revealed to Jesus that the father had a glimmer of hope that Jesus could do what he had asked.

The father's next words, "if there's anything you can do . . . ," elicited a strong response from Jesus. Jesus repeated the father's words back to him, almost as if to say, *Are you kidding Me? If! Of course I can!* Of course Jesus can. He has all authority in heaven and on earth. He is the Healer. He had healed many people before this young man and would heal many after. It is consistent with His character. It is consistent with His spoken word.

Jesus' answer to this father could not have been clearer: "All things are possible, if you only believe" (Mark 9:23).

Oh, friend, I want you to hear Jesus' words loud and clear. Savor them. Digest them.

Not just anything but *everything* is possible in Jesus. There are no limits with God! When you pray, pray with full belief that He is able.

The quandary is that sometimes what we ask is not what He wills. But He is *always* able.

Jesus' words to the father were enough for him to take another step of faith.

What were the father's next words to Jesus in Mark 9:24? How long did it take him to come to this conclusion?

Jesus had spoken truth into the father's heart and mind. And as he looked into Jesus' eyes, the father believed. He wanted to believe 100 percent, but he wasn't quite there, so he cried out, "I believe, Lord. Help me to believe!" (Mark 9:24).

Positionally, this is where Jesus wants us when we pray. He wants us to pray in faith, believing He is able (James 1:5–7). And when the evil one tries to plant seeds of doubt, He wants us to cry out for His help so that we can take every negative thought, every doubting thought, and every lie captive and replace it with truth. (2 Corinthians 10:5).

Read the following statement:

What makes faith valid is not its subjective strength, but the trustworthiness of its object.

Read it again.

What makes faith valid is not its subjective strength, but the trustworthiness of its object.[9]

Emotionally, our faith is often muddled by fear, hesitancy, and doubt. But our feelings become irrelevant when Jesus is the object of our faith—when He alone is the One in whom we trust . . . not ourselves, not our emotions, not our abilities . . . but Him alone.

Hebrews 11:6 says, "Without faith no one can please God because the one coming to God must believe He exists, and He rewards those who come seeking." When you doubt God is listening, when you doubt He is at work, remember the truths we have studied today. Jesus knows our weaknesses because He walked on this earth as one of us. He desires that His children have a deep and abiding faith, so when we pray, He will supply what we lack. He also promises, according to this verse, to reward those who earnestly seek Him.

> Faith does not just happen. We must cultivate it.

The disciples failed in their efforts probably because they had neglected prayer and preparation. The authority Jesus had given them was still effective. But it was not effective for them in that moment because they had failed to prepare their hearts and minds to do that which Jesus had authorized them to do. Faith does not just happen. We must cultivate it. We must engage in spiritual disciplines, like praying, studying, and fasting. The disciples' failure to perform this healing frustrated Jesus. He knew it was because they had been careless with their faith.

There are so many times I have been careless with my faith, careless with my choices. That carelessness exacerbated the messiness in my life.

What about you? Are you careless with your faith? Do you neglect studying the Word? Do you neglect prayer?

Listen to this amazing promise from John 14:13:

> Whatever you ask for in My name, I will do it **so that** the Father will get glory from the Son. (Bold emphasis added)

Does this verse teach that whatever we pray in Jesus' name, we get? No, it doesn't. The first part of this verse, "Whatever you ask for in My name, I will do," is not a magic formula. Praying in Jesus' name does not guarantee that God will deliver. Praying in Jesus' name means something far different. It means that we are asking God for something that aligns with His will, something that would please Him, something that would bring Him glory and further His kingdom on earth.

Read 1 John 5:14–15. Write these verses in your own words. How do they confirm our "so that" verse?

It's like when my daughter interviewed for a job. She had a friend with a connection at the company where she was interviewing. Her friend told her to feel free to use her name. By offering this, Lauren's friend was granting her the privilege of using her name. And although her friend's name meant something because she had once worked there, Lauren still had to do her part. She had to research the company, understand their needs, and sell what she could bring to the job. Using her friend's name alone carried with it no guarantee that she would get the job.

The same is true when we pray in Jesus' name. Speaking His name is not enough. We must understand His nature and character. We must know God's will. The goal of prayer must be to honor God and His name, not ourselves.

What is the "so that" in John 14:13? What does this mean?

Do you know what it means when we pray in Jesus' name? We are standing before God in Jesus' place. We are pleading before the Father not because of who we are but because of who Jesus is. And God answers prayers prayed in Jesus' name when they are prayers that fall within His will and will glorify Him and Him alone. They are not self-centered. They are God-centered. That does not mean they cannot be prayers for ourselves and our loved ones, but we must examine the motives of our hearts.

Isn't it amazing that the God of the universe desires to use us to do His kingdom work? At one time, Jesus was God's agent on earth, but now we are His agents. He wants to do powerful things in and through us! Just as God empowered Jesus, He will empower us. The fact that God chooses to use ordinary people like you and me to do extraordinary things on this earth brings Him even greater glory (John 14:12)!

Friend, we have enormous spiritual power coursing through our veins. These are the questions we must ask: Do we believe it? Do we understand it? Do we access it? And, finally, do we pray for it to become powerful and effective in our prayers and in our lives?

For most of us, the answer is no. Writing this lesson convicted me to cry out for more of His power in my prayer life. I want Him to fan the flames of my faith to greater heights! I want to be used to do the "even greater things" He mentioned in John 14:12 because He has gone to be with the Father.

At the beginning of this section, you answered questions about your prayer life. Now that you have studied prayer and its role in giving you a bolder faith, will you make changes in your prayer life? If you answered yes, share what step(s) you will take, and write a prayer committing this to the Lord.

CONCLUDING THOUGHTS:

God made His power available to us through the indwelling of His Holy Spirit. This is a precious gift that belongs only to God's children. The Spirit of the living God lives in us. God desires that we be filled to the full with that presence. But we have a role in this. We can either quench His Spirit or we can be filled to overflowing. The choice is ours.

We must *actively pray* for His Spirit to invade every part of our being. When we truly invite Him to fill us and use us, the supernatural experiences He will grant us . . . the ways He will use us . . . will blow our minds!

As we end today, my prayer is that we would daily pursue a Spirit-filled, Christ-empowered life . . . a life Jesus can use to bring hope and healing to His broken and hurting world. May God receive all the praise, glory, and honor for the fruits that result from this prayer! Show us your glory, Lord; show us your glory!

Based on how God has spoken to your heart, complete the thought below.

Pray so that . . .

PART FIVE:
Remain in Him

MEMORY VERSE: LET US THEN APPROACH THE THRONE OF GRACE WITH CONFIDENCE, **SO THAT** WE MAY RECEIVE MERCY AND FIND GRACE TO HELP US IN OUR TIME OF NEED.

–Hebrews 4:16 (NIV; emphasis added)

Today we rejoin Jesus on His walk with His disciples to the Garden of Gethsemane. Our last "so that" comes directly from the lips of Jesus as He tells His disciples that He is the True Vine. Their walk takes them past a vineyard where they are able to see an abundance of vines bursting forth with fruit. Imagine you are walking along with them as Jesus speaks these words:

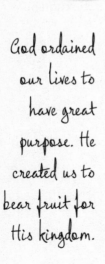

God ordained our lives to have great purpose. He created us to bear fruit for His kingdom.

If you remain in me and my words remain in you, ask whatever you wish, and it will be given you. This is to my Father's glory, *[so] that* you bear much fruit, showing yourselves to be my disciples. (John 15:7–8 NIV; emphasis added)

God ordained our lives to have great purpose. He created us to bear fruit for His kingdom. He wants to answer our prayers so that we can make a difference in His world, and He equips us to do just that.

Satan, on the other hand, wants nothing more than for us to believe we are insignificant. He lies when he says that only a chosen few—the great preachers and teachers—have true value in the eyes of God. He whispers lies, saying that we are unworthy because of what we have done or what has been done to us. "God could never use *you*."

Friend, if those lies were true, God would never have sacrificed His one and only Son for you. Jesus willingly gave His life on the cross because He loves and values *you*. In John 15:9, Jesus says, "As the Father has loved me, so have I loved you. Now remain in my love" (NIV).

God loves us as much as He loves His only begotten Son. God's love for His Son is reflected in the words He spoke in Matthew 3:17 when John baptized Jesus: "This is My Son, **whom I love**; . . . with Him I am well pleased" (bold emphasis added).

Jesus has this same love for us, and this love is inexhaustible. It is unmatched by any love we have ever known. Jesus died and rose again to lavish this love upon us.

After expressing the magnitude of His love for them, Jesus told His disciples to remain in His love.

What does it look like to "remain" in Jesus' love?

What keeps you from "remaining" in Jesus' love?

Friend, Take a few minutes to soak in His love. Let all that He has done for you wash over you each and every day. Remind yourself that *your* Savior did the following:

- died for *you* (John 3:16)

- loves *you* with an everlasting love (Jeremiah 31:3)

- delights in *you* (Psalm 147:11)
- calls *you* the apple of His eye (Zechariah 2:8)
- promises to never fail *you* or abandon *you* (Deuteronomy 31:6)
- has written *your* name on the palm of His hand (Isaiah 49:16)
- crowns *you* with unfailing love and compassion (Psalm 103:4)

Whenever the devil, the father of lies, brings his accusations, his discouragement, and his fear against you, relentlessly speak these truths over yourself. Walk confidently because *you* are God's beloved.

And then . . . remain in that love.

→→→ APPLICATION:

Practically, what does it look like to remain in Christ's love? Jesus' choice of words and the geographical location of their walk offer a beautiful picture of remaining.

The key to remaining in God's love is time. We must spend *time* with Jesus. Just as the branches upon which the disciples looked as they walked past the vineyard were connected to the vine, we too must remain connected to Christ. The vine provided the branches with sap, the vital nutrients they needed to grow. Similarly, Christ, the True Vine, provides sap. I call it Holy Spirit sap, the vital nutrients we need to grow and mature as children of God.

Let's look at the first part of our verse from John 15:7: "If you remain in me and my words remain in you . . ." (NIV). The Voice translation uses the word "abide." Abiding or remaining in Christ means spending time in His presence and in His written Word. As we allow the Word to permeate our hearts and minds, it becomes a part of us. God's Holy Spirit sap, the fruit of His Spirit from Galatians 5—love, joy, peace, patience, kindheartedness, goodness, faithfulness, gentleness, self-control—becomes fully alive in us. As each fruit grows bigger and stronger, we become more fruitful. Making faith-filled choices becomes easier. We become the kind of people Jesus can use to impact the kingdom. We are His agents, who shine light into darkness; offer hope in hopelessness; provide joy in sadness; bring unity to division, and healing to hurt.

John 15:7 continues, ". . . ask whatever you wish, and it will be given you" (NIV).

This verse must be read in light of the rest of John 15 about fruit bearing. Receiving whatever we wish requires a close, intimate, interactive relationship with Christ. It is in that place of intimacy that we will hear God's voice and find His will. Our prayers will change from being me-centered to God-centered and others-centered. The motives behind our prayers will change because our hearts have changed.

Our fruit bearing is directly proportional to our abiding. We will see our prayers answered more and more as our abiding increases more and more.

We will see our prayers answered more and more as our abiding increases more and more.

Examine the fruit of the Spirit listed above. Choose one fruit God has grown in your life. Share how He has used that fruit through prayer and abiding to show His love and encouragement to others.

Choose one fruit of the Spirit with which you struggle (if you are like me, there may be many, but choose one). Why is it difficult to allow God to grow this fruit in you? What are some steps you can take to grow this fruit?

There is one more important truth related to remaining in Christ's love. Jesus says in John 15:10:

"If you obey my commands, you will remain in my love, just as I have obeyed my Father's commands and remain in his love." (NIV)

What is the prerequisite to remaining in His love?

We are called to obedience. Jesus walked in perfect obedience to the will of the Father. He only did what He heard the Father tell Him. He never once stepped outside His Father's will, even unto death.

God requires a heart of obedience as a prerequisite to bearing abundant fruit. We cannot draw near to God with a rebellious heart. He is holy and cannot be in the presence of a child whose heart is hostile toward Him. Oh, please don't hear me saying that He doesn't love us if we are rebellious and hostile. He always loves us, and that never changes. But what I am saying is we will not be able to draw near to Him. We will not be able to hear His voice.

I want you to fully understand this relationship between love and obedience and fruit bearing, so let's review for a moment.

a. What must we do to *keep* God's love?

b. What must we do to bear fruit?

Listen carefully. The first question is a trick question. We need not do anything to keep God's love. God's love is not based on our efforts. Because we are His children, He lavishes His love on us without condition. We did nothing to earn it, and we are not required to do anything to keep it. It's crazy, but true!

But bearing fruit is different. Our fruit bearing *is* measured by *our* efforts. First, we must know the love we have in Christ and live in its fullness. Second, we must know the source from which wisdom and power come, and we must connect with that source and remain in it. Third, we must listen to what we hear and then obey.

There is a progression. It doesn't happen all at once. Initially, we may bear little or no fruit. As time passes and we experience God's presence, recognize His voice, and grow in wisdom and knowledge, fruit bearing increases. Then as we experience God more deeply, step out in prayer, and allow Him to use us more, we will bear even more fruit. God's goal, my friend, is that we bear much fruit . . . exceedingly, abundantly more fruit than we could ever ask or imagine! (See Ephesians 3:20.)

IF YOU WANT TO GO DEEPER:

Let's end our time with Jesus' words and our final "so that" in John 15:11:

> I have told you this *so that* my joy may be in you and that your joy may be complete. (NIV; emphasis added)

Friend, John 15 gives us the recipe for joy. We receive joy one way and one way only . . . a Holy Spirit transfusion. As we abide in the Vine, Christ infuses us with a fresh filling of His Spirit. During this infusion, *His* nature flows into us.

Read Galatians 5:22–23. Of what does God's nature consist?

We become less and He becomes more. In the beginning, He apportions each fruit equally. As we abide and obey, our fruit begins to grow, at different rates and at different times. God then opens doors for us to use that fruit . . . to step out in prayer and interact with others so that we bear fruit in ways that will bless others and allow His kingdom to grow. Abiding and obeying gives our lives purpose because it is in the midst of these activities that God works in and through us to do His work.

This, sweet friend, is the key to a joy-filled, fruit-filled life!

Read Ephesians 3:16–19:

> *Father,* out of Your *honorable and* glorious riches, strengthen Your people. Fill their souls with the power of Your Spirit **so that** through faith the Anointed One will reside in their hearts. May love be *the rich soil* where their lives take root. May it be the bedrock where their lives are founded *so that together* with all of Your people they will have the power to understand that the love of the Anointed is infinitely long, wide, high, and deep, surpassing everything anyone previously experienced. God, may Your fullness flood through their entire beings. (Bold emphasis added)

Paul prays two prayers in his letter to the church in Ephesus. We studied a passage from the first prayer in Part Three. This is a portion of the second prayer. Paul prays the first prayer so that we might know the blessings we have in Christ. He prays this second prayer so that we may be strengthened, filled, and empowered to actively walk in those blessings. Now that we know our blessings and how to access them, Paul prays that we might put them to work in our daily lives.

Consider our lesson and break apart Ephesians 3:16–19 just as we did our other "so that" verses. Spend time with the Lord, asking Him to teach you what He wants you to take from this passage.

Now that we know our blessings and how to access them, Paul prays that we might put them to work in our daily lives.

⟶⟶ CONCLUDING THOUGHTS:

There is only one way to learn how to pray more effectively, and that is to "just do it."

⟶⟶ MY CALL TO ACTION:

If you are not comfortable with praying, take baby steps. Choose one area we have studied and apply it in your prayer life. Maybe you need to really know and understand God loves you. Search for verses on His love, study them, and even memorize them. Keep them close to your heart until you feel His love seep into the depths of your soul.

Maybe you struggle with abiding. Set aside a short time with God each day with no agenda (maybe three to five minutes). For example, open your Bible to the book of Psalms and read for just a few minutes. Begin to pray some of the psalms back to God, personalizing them with "I" and "me." Get a little notebook or journal and record what you learn, hear, and feel as you remain in Him.

If you already have a daily prayer life, apply what you have learned in these chapters and take it to the next level. Take areas in your life (or people) and search for verses that speak to those areas. Study the verses and personalize them for your situation. Commit to pray each verse, fully believing that God will work in and through them just as He promises. Invite Him to be at work, and look for Him to be at work. Anticipate His work. Journal what you learn, hear, and feel through this process.

If you are struggling with how to take the next step, here are a few examples:

- If you have circumstances right now that seem impossible, remember God promises in His Word that *all things are possible* (Luke 18:27).

- If you feel you are overcommitted and so tired that you cannot take another step, remember God promises that *He will give you rest* and *you can do all things through Him who strengthens you* (Matthew 11:28–30; Philippians 4:13).

- If you feel lost and confused and don't know what direction to take, remember God gives you a formula that shows you how He will *direct your steps* (Proverbs 3:5–6).

- If you hold tightly to things from the past, things for which you cannot forgive yourself, remember God's promise: *I forgive you* (1 John 1:9; Romans 8:1).

- If you worry about your finances or how you will make ends meet, remember God promises *He will supply all your needs* (Philippians 4:19).

- If you fear what the future holds for your husband, your marriage, your children, or your job, remember *He has not given you a spirit of fear, but of power and of love and of a sound mind* (2 Timothy 1:7 NKJV).

> *If you have circumstances right now that seem impossible, remember God promises in His Word that all things are possible.*

I share these verses as a starting point. Take the verse given and search for more using key words and the concordance in the back of your Bible. Use the notes for each verse found in your margins and at the bottom of each page. Pray for the Lord to lead you through His Word.

I am praying for you, sweet friend . . . praying for God to do big things!

CHAPTER FOUR

Trials Come So That...

MEMORY VERSE: CONSIDER IT PURE JOY, MY BROTHERS, WHENEVER YOU FACE TRIALS OF MANY KINDS, BECAUSE YOU KNOW THAT THE TESTING OF YOUR FAITH DEVELOPS PERSEVERANCE. PERSEVERANCE MUST FINISH ITS WORK **SO THAT** YOU MAY BE MATURE AND COMPLETE, NOT LACKING ANYTHING.

—James 1:2–4 (NIV; emphasis added)

PRAYER:

This prayer is from Psalm 62:1–8 (NLT):

I wait quietly before God,
    for my victory comes from Him.
He alone is my rock and my salvation,
    my fortress where I will never be shaken.

So many enemies against one man—
    all of them trying to kill me.

To them I'm just a broken-down wall
    or a tottering fence.
They plan to topple me from my high position.
    They delight in telling lies about me.
They praise me to my face
    but curse me in their hearts. *Interlude*

Let all that I am wait quietly before God,
    for my hope is in Him.
He alone is my rock and my salvation,
    my fortress where I will not be shaken.
My victory and honor come from God alone.
    He is my refuge, a rock where no enemy can reach me.
O my people, trust in Him at all times.
    Pour out your heart to Him,
    for God is our refuge.

PART ONE:
Why Does God Allow Trials?

I learned firsthand circumstances come into our lives that can destroy everything we know to be good and true. "It was June of 1986, just days after my college graduation. I walked into my home to find an armed, masked man standing at the top of my stairs. The afternoon he spent in my apartment transformed my life forever. Even as I write this, it takes me back to a desperate time and reminds me of the years of terror, despair and hopelessness in which I lived."[1]

For the days and months following my attack, I shook my fist at God, asking, *How could You sit on Your throne in heaven and allow the horrible things that man did to me?* Night after night I lay in my bed, tears soaking my pillow. Questions plagued my mind. *Why didn't You protect me? Why didn't You warn me? Why did You abandon me?* Well-meaning friends would tell me that God had a purpose, that He would bring good out of it. I knew they meant well. But how could they utter such ridiculous statements? No good would ever come from what happened to me that day. What possible purpose could there be for the vile acts that man committed against me?

This chapter of our study addresses what God's Word has to say on why bad things happen to God's people. You see, at the time I was raped, I was unfamiliar with the Bible. Oh, I had read it now and again, but I didn't know God's Word. I didn't know that the Bible spoke to the very questions I was asking, not once, but many

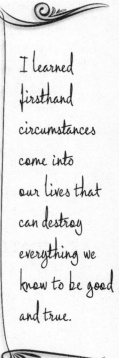

I learned firsthand circumstances come into our lives that can destroy everything we know to be good and true.

times. Once God equipped me with the truths and promises found in His Word, understanding and healing came.

Being equipped with truth enables us to face our trials from an entirely different perspective. How I wish I'd had that perspective in June 1986. But I'm certain if I had, I wouldn't be writing these words today.

We begin today in the book of James:

> Consider it pure joy, my brothers, whenever you face trials of many kinds, because you know that the testing of your faith develops perseverance. Perseverance must finish its work *so that* you may be mature and complete, not lacking anything. (1:2–4 NIV; emphasis added)

Before we dive into our topic for today, I want to share a bit of background on James. James, like John, wrote his letter so that people's faith would increase. But James was not as concerned with a "saving" faith as he was a "practical" faith. Consequently, his letter teaches his audience how to live out their Christian faith in everyday life.

Like the author of Hebrews, James wrote to the Hebrew Christians, people who had lived under the Old Testament law but had since come to know Jesus and given their lives to Him. Some refer to the book of James as the New Testament equivalent of the book of Proverbs.

APPLICATION:

I don't know about you, but when adversity hits, my first response is not usually, *Thank You, God. How do You want to use this in my life?* Instead, you'll probably hear me groaning and complaining. Rather than looking for God in the midst of my difficulties, often I'm looking for a way out.

James 1:2–4 gives sound advice and a fresh perspective on trials. Let's do a bit of word history before we begin. It's imperative that we understand how the word "trials" is used in this context. Sometimes looking to another translation is helpful. James 1:2 in the King James Version says, "My brethren, count it all joy when ye fall into divers temptations."

The Greek word translated *divers* means "various, varicolored." To give insight into its meaning, one commentator wrote, "My wife and I once visited a world-famous weaver and watched his men and women work on the looms. I noticed that the undersides of the rugs were not very beautiful: the patterns were obscure and the loose ends of yarn dangled. 'Don't judge the worker or the work by looking at the wrong side,' our guide told us. In the same way, we are looking at the wrong side of life; only the Lord sees the finished pattern. Let's not judge Him or His work from what we see today. His work is not finished yet!"[2]

God alone can take that tangled mess and weave it together to create a beautiful masterpiece intentionally and intricately woven together for His glory.

Don't you just love that visual? Weavers use all sorts of colors and patterns to create their finished product, and it's the weaving together of the colored yarn in intricate patterns that creates a beautiful, unique end product.

Our trials, like the yarns the weaver uses to make the rug, are not all alike. What we see with our eyes looks chaotic and unsettled and, in fact, may feel like a huge, tangled mess. God alone can take that tangled mess and weave it together to create a beautiful masterpiece intentionally and intricately woven together for His glory.

The Greek word translated *peirasmos* means both "trial" and "temptation." These are trials that have a beneficiary purpose. They are allowed and shaped by God to strengthen our faith and enhance our lives.

Some trials come from within due to choices we have made. Others come from outside ourselves. Give examples of each of these trials in your own life.

In verse 2, what word follows "Consider it pure joy, my brothers"? Why is this word choice significant?

James did not choose the word "if." He chose the word "when." It's not a matter of *whether* trials will come but *when* trials will come. Trials are inevitable because we are fallen people and we live in a fallen world (1 Thessalonians 3:3). So, my friend, if we know trials will come, we don't need to waste time asking God, *Why me? What did I do to deserve this?* Our questions should change. *God, will You help me walk through this trial? How do You want to use this in my life?*

God knows that when our trials come, we will have questions and want answers. And, being a good God, He doesn't leave us without answers. Through His Word, He provides guiding truths and principles to teach us how to walk through our trials with faith and hope.

Walking through trials is a process. First, we must examine the type of trial we are experiencing. Is it one we have brought upon ourselves as a consequence of our own choices? Or is it one that the Lord has allowed to refine us?

TRIALS CAUSED BY OUR CHOICES:

When a trial comes because of a choice we have made, we must ask God how we have disobeyed or rebelled against Him.

We make choices every day. Some are good. But some are bad and lead to very unpleasant consequences. One of the greatest biblical examples we find of a really bad choice is in the life of King David when he committed adultery with Bathsheba (2 Samuel 11). He chose to commit adultery with the wife of one of his soldiers. His decision led to terrible consequences, both personally and professionally.

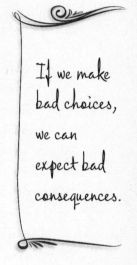

If we make bad choices, we can expect bad consequences.

Another example is Jonah. He disobeyed the call he heard from the Lord to go to Nineveh (Jonah 1). Defying God's call was his choice, and it led to life-altering consequences.

Galatians 6:7 says, "Do not be deceived: God cannot be mocked. A man reaps what he sows" (NIV). The biblical law of sowing and reaping is still in effect. If we make good choices, we can expect good consequences. If we make bad choices, we can expect bad consequences.

This sounds logical, right?

But sometimes we cannot see this in our own circumstances. Take marriage, for example. Let me share a little story with you.

I had just cleaned my kitchen . . . everything perfect and in its place . . . counters shining, stovetop sparkling. And then it happened. Within moments of completing this labor of love, my husband walked through the door.

I should have been thrilled, but I wasn't. I knew what was coming. He was home for lunch and was going to create one of the gourmet sandwiches he loves to make. All I could think about was the grease that would soon be on my freshly polished stove and the dishes that would soon fill my sink.

My mind went right to the mess he was about to make in *my* freshly cleaned kitchen. I couldn't stand it, so I launched into a series of instructions:

"Please don't make a mess. I just cleaned."

"Please put your dishes in the dishwasher."

"Please wipe your crumbs off the counter."

"Please clean the stove I spent an hour scrubbing."

I was polite. Did you count my "pleases"? I just have a way I like things to be done in my kitchen . . . my way.

I saw the look on his face. I knew what he was thinking: *You have got to be kidding me. Did she really just say that? Why did I even come home for lunch?*

I realized I was nagging. I knew I was being controlling. And this wasn't the first time.

Often after I speak such words, I find myself asking, *Did I really just say that?*

Friend, if we continually nag and berate our husbands, we will alienate them. Our houses will become battle zones. Our marriages will feel empty and lifeless. In reality, our words and actions lead to those consequences. I have learned that if I'm not willing to humble myself and admit my fault, I'll blame my husband. I'll whine and complain: *Why is my marriage so miserable? Why does my husband not treat me with respect? Why doesn't my husband listen to me and care what I say?*

God allows us to live with the consequences of our sinful choices. And the only way out of this cycle is to be in the Word so that we can recognize our sin. Once we recognize it, God can forgive us and lead us to right living.

In my marriage example, my own choices led to my kitchen being a battle zone that day. I knew my behavior was wrong.

I don't want to be a control freak. After each incident like this (and there have been many), I promise myself no matter what—dishes in the sink, crumbs on the counter, grease on the stove—I won't say anything.

The truth is, it is not who I am. It is who I am used to being.

But inevitably, I fail. It may be hours later or days later, but the opportunity arises again to hold my tongue, and I blow it once more. Within minutes, the words start spewing.

I'm convinced my way is best. Deep inside, I know I should not be this way, but then I hear that voice of justification: *It's just who I am.*

The truth is, it is *not* who I am. It is who I am *used to being.*

But it's not who God wants me to be. In fact, His Word tells me exactly how He wants me to respond with my speech. My words should be:

- **Edifying:** "Don't let even one rotten word seep out of your mouths. Instead, offer only fresh words that build others up when they need it most" (Ephesians 4:29).

- **Gentle:** "A tender answer turns away rage, but a prickly reply spikes anger" (Proverbs 15:1).

- **Self-controlled:** "A fool *does not think before he* unleashes his temper, but a wise man holds back *and remains quiet*" (Proverbs 29:11).

- **Compassionate:** "Instead, be kind and compassionate. *Graciously* forgive one another just as God has forgiven you through the Anointed, *our Liberating King*" (Ephesians 4:32).

But, friend, we will not know these truths if we are not in the Word. And living these truths is so hard to do on our own! The good news is that we don't have to live them on our own. God enables us to walk in obedience to these scriptures through the power of His Holy Spirit. He will mold us and make us more like Him. And on those days when we feel as if there is no way we can speak kindly to others, let's remember His Word says we can do *all* things through Christ who strengthens us (Philippians 4:13).

Friend, when we quiet our hearts, when we open His Word instead of our mouths, when we approach Him with a heart of surrender, when we choose to submit to His ways instead of our own . . . *that* is when God will do His work and help us to hold our tongues and choose our words carefully.

Trials of our own doing quite often arise because of our choices. Our choices make or break relationships . . . especially in marriage and parenting. In my marriage example, it was my responsibility to stop the pattern of behavior that brought about the arguing and isolation in the first place. My words and my actions determined the consequences. Remember, we reap what we sow.

TRIALS AUTHORED BY GOD'S HAND:

What about the suffering we endure that is not due to our own choices? This is the hardest suffering to understand. Scripture teaches that God sometimes does send trials and difficulties into the lives of His children for a purpose. How do we understand suffering that comes from the hand of God?

How can a good God be the author of pain and suffering? We need only study the life of Joseph to understand (Genesis 37–50).

Joseph's brothers sold him into slavery. He was taken to Egypt, framed for a crime he did not commit, unjustly convicted, and sentenced to prison. Don't you think Joseph wondered what God was doing? Yet, throughout his years in Egypt, Joseph trusted God. He did the best he could with his circumstances. He stayed close to God. He prayed. And years later, God gave him the answer. He finally saw God's purpose in his years of suffering. God needed Joseph in Egypt in the pharaoh's house to save the Israelites from a terrible famine. Joseph not only saw God's purpose but also testified to it when he forgave his brothers for what they did: "Even though you intended to harm me, God intended it only for good, and through me, He preserved the lives of countless people, as He is still doing today" (Genesis 50:20).

Job serves as another great example. In the first chapter of Job, the Lord initiated a conversation with Satan. That dialogue led to the testing of Job. God held Job up as a righteous man. Satan claimed that Job's righteousness was meaningless because God had richly blessed him and placed a hedge of protection around him. Satan contended that if God took away all Job had, he would curse God to His face. God responded with these words:

> "Very well, then, everything he has is in your power, but on the man himself do not lay a finger." (Job 1:12 NIV)

God gave Satan permission to afflict Job. But God limited what Satan could do.

These are not the only two stories from Scripture that speak of God as the author of suffering.

Joseph not only saw God's purpose but also testified to it when he forgave his brothers for what they did.

🖋 **Read Psalm 119:67, 71, 75; and Hebrews 12:5–11.** Share what you learn.

🖋 How does this make you feel about God? Why?

It's difficult to think of God this way. But we must remember that He is our Creator *and* our Father. He knows us inside and out and always has our best interests at heart, just as loving, caring parents always have a child's best interests at heart. God allows trials for many reasons. Sometimes He needs to refine us to make us more like Him. Sometimes He seeks to strengthen our faith. And sometimes another person may need to see Christ's character demonstrated in us in order to grow his or her own faith. One promise of which we can be certain . . . when we respond to trials with faith and trust, God will use our suffering for good, and it will point people to God and bring glory to Him.

🖋 **Reread James 1:2–4.**

Consider it pure joy, my brothers, whenever you face trials of many kinds, because you know that the testing of your faith develops perseverance. Perseverance must finish its work *so that* you may be mature and complete, not lacking anything. (NIV; emphasis added)

🪶 With what kind of attitude are we to approach our trials?

🪶 What does Peter say in 1 Peter 4:12–13 about how we should respond to suffering?

When a trial arises, we have a choice as to how we will handle it. James tells us we are to "consider it pure joy . . . whenever [we] face trials of many kinds" (1:2 NIV). The King James Version says we are to "count it all joy." This word "count" means "evaluate." When trials come, we must evaluate them in light of God's truths and promises. It's not the trial itself that we consider a joy. Rather, the *results* that will come from the trial are what we consider pure joy. Hebrews 12:2 tells us that Jesus endured the cross because of the "joy that was set before Him." He knew He would be resurrected and would ascend to once again sit at the right hand of His Father in heaven. And He knew one day He would return to get His bride.

🪶 According to James 1:2–4, why are we to consider our trials pure joy?

The testing of our faith produces perseverance (v. 3 NIV). "Perseverance" is a translation of the Greek word *hupomone*, which means "an abiding under." As used here, it means steadfastness or endurance in the face of difficulties. This is not a passive acceptance of our circumstances. It is courageous persevering to reach what is promised on the other side.

Listen to Paul's words in Romans 5:3–4:

> Not only so, but we also rejoice in our sufferings, because we know that suffering produces perseverance; perseverance, character; and character, hope. (NIV)

We cannot learn endurance by reading a devotional, listening to a sermon, or praying a prayer. We must walk through a trial, trusting and obeying God every step of the way. I have never forgotten these words from a woman who had walked through more trials than one person should ever have to endure:

> "God's faithfulness is *most effectively learned* when experienced."

Complete James 1:4, using the NIV's rendering as your guide: "Perseverance must finish its work so that you may be _____ and _____ , not lacking anything.

What do you think James means by "mature" and "complete"?

Time and time again, God's Word reveals that before God can work *through* us, He must do a work *in* us.

Fill in the blanks from the statement above. "Before God can work _____ us, He must do a work _____ us."

God spent decades working *in* the lives of Abraham, Joseph, Moses, and David before He ever worked *through* them. God built David's character before He called him to be king. He humbled Paul's heart before He called him to be one of the greatest evangelists that walked the earth. Jesus' disciples suffered trials and experienced tests before Jesus sent them out "to all the earth." God refines us through our suffering.

Perseverance builds character. The NIV describes that character as "mature and complete." The King James Version says "perfect and entire." The Greek word for "perfect" is *telos* and means "finished, wanting nothing necessary to completeness, perfect." It implies a mature faith confidently lived out in the midst of everyday life.

The Greek word for "complete" is *holokleros* and means "complete in every part, perfectly sound." It speaks of the health and wholeness of our bodies, physically and spiritually. Our hearts, minds, and spirits come into perfect unity just as the Father, Son, and Holy Spirit live in perfect unity.

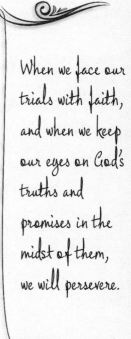

When we face our trials with faith, and when we keep our eyes on God's truths and promises in the midst of them, we will persevere.

When we face our trials with faith, and when we keep our eyes on God's truths and promises in the midst of them, we will persevere. Each step of courageous perseverance builds on the next until we each come out the other side a thoroughly mature believer, not lacking anything.

IF YOU WANT TO GO DEEPER:

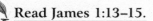

Read James 1:13–15.

The same Greek root lies behind the word "trials" in James 1:2 (NIV) and the word "tempted" here. But the emphasis in James 1:2–3 is on difficulties that come from outside ourselves. In verses 13–15, James focuses on temptations that come from within.

✎ Give examples of "inward" temptations.

James makes it abundantly clear that God is never the author of sin. God cannot tempt because, by His very nature, He is holy. It follows that He cannot tempt anyone to sin. He cannot promote something that is repugnant to His nature.

Satan is the author of sin. Jesus tells us that he is the "father of lies" (John 8:44). Matthew calls Satan "the tempter" (Matthew 4:3).

God tests us to bring about the best in us. Satan tempts us to bring out the worst in us. So please know that God is never the source of temptation. Satan tempts us by appealing to our inner man, our flesh.

✎ Explain the progression of sin described in James 1:14–15.

✎ Where along the way should we stop this progression, and what steps should we take to do so?

Friend, this is why Paul tells us in 2 Corinthians 10:5:

We are demolishing arguments and ideas, every high-and-mighty philosophy that pits itself against the knowledge of *the one true God*. We are taking prisoners of every thought, *every emotion,* and subduing them into obedience to the Anointed One.

Share ways you can take negative thoughts captive.

Read Philippians 4:8. With what does Paul tell us to replace those thoughts? Give some examples.

CONCLUDING THOUGHTS:

We have spent significant time in James 1:2–4. Based on how God has spoken to your heart, complete the thought below.

Trials come so that . . .

living so that ❧

PART TWO:
God's All-Sufficient Grace

MEMORY VERSE: CONSIDER IT PURE JOY, MY BROTHERS,
WHENEVER YOU FACE TRIALS OF MANY KINDS, BECAUSE
YOU KNOW THAT THE TESTING OF YOUR FAITH DEVELOPS
PERSEVERANCE. PERSEVERANCE MUST FINISH ITS WORK **SO THAT**
YOU MAY BE MATURE AND COMPLETE, NOT LACKING ANYTHING.

–James 1:2-4 (NIV; emphasis added)

Remember to take time to work on your memory verse. This is a powerful verse to keep in your arsenal of truth for the times when trials come into your life or into the life of someone you love.

Today we will spend time in one of Paul's most well-known passages from 2 Corinthians, specifically the "so that" verse of 2 Corinthians 12:9:

> But he said to me, "My grace is sufficient for you, for my power is made perfect in weakness." Therefore I will boast all the more gladly about my weaknesses, *so that* Christ's power may rest on me. (NIV; emphasis added)

 Read 2 Corinthians 12:1-10.

➡➡ APPLICATION:

As we learned in Part One, God sometimes uses suffering in our lives as a tool to build godly character. In the midst of refining us, He pours out His amazing grace. Paul effectively portrays this truth in this passage from 2 Corinthians.

Paul begins this portion of Scripture by sharing a vision in which he was "caught up into paradise" (12:3). His experience had occurred years before, and even Paul was not certain exactly what had happened. But he knew his spirit had risen to a place where he was in the presence of God. What he learned, Scripture says, he could not tell. But I cannot help but wonder if God gave him not only a glimpse of paradise but also a personal word to prepare Paul for all the trials and tribulations that lay ahead for him and his ministry. In 2 Corinthians 4:16–17 Paul wrote:

> So we have no reason to despair. Despite the fact that our outer humanity is falling apart and decaying, our inner humanity is breathing in new life every day. You see, the short-lived pains of this life are creating for us an eternal glory that does not compare to anything we know here.

Had God warned Paul during his trip to paradise of the impending thorn in his side? Did God impart truths and promises that would sustain him? We will never know for certain, but I would like to think so.

What reason does Paul give in verse 7 for his thorn in the flesh?

How does reading this make you feel about God?

Paul says outright that God allowed this thorn in the flesh to keep him from being conceited, and he called this thorn "a messenger of Satan" (NIV).

2 Corinthians 12:7 in the King James Version reads:

And lest I should be exalted above measure through the abundance of the revelations, there was given to me a thorn in the flesh, the messenger of Satan to buffet me, lest I should be exalted above measure.

As hard as it is to understand, there is no other way to read Paul's words. Paul had gone to paradise and back . . . an experience few are given. God abhors pride. He knows it leads to deeper temptation and to sin. God knew Paul's frame and inclinations, and perhaps because of this, He gave him this thorn to keep him from becoming prideful about his incredible experience. Without it, perhaps the fourteen years of ministry that followed Paul's visit to paradise would have been filled with failure instead of success.

It's interesting to note that Scripture does not identify this thorn. The word translated "thorn" is *skolops* and means "anything pointed." Another commentary translates it as "a sharp stake used for torturing or impaling someone."[3] What seems clear is that it indicates a physical affliction of some kind that brings great pain and distress. There are many theories, but none proven. Some believe it was epilepsy, others an eye ailment, and still others severe headaches. For our teaching purposes, it really doesn't matter. In fact, I think it is best we not know because then, no matter what our suffering may be, we are able to look to Paul's experience for wisdom and encouragement.

> God abhors pride. He knows it leads to deeper temptation and to sin.

Just as it's hard to understand how God permitted Satan to afflict Job, it's hard to understand why He allowed Satan to afflict Paul. Both were godly men walking in obedience to what God had called them to do.

My research and study revealed no definitive answer. But I find comfort in God's words to the prophet, Isaiah: "My intentions are not *always* yours, and I do not go about things as you do. My thoughts and My ways are above and beyond you, just as heaven is far from your reach here on earth" (Isaiah 55:8–9).

We know there is evil in our world; we see it all around us every day. We know God has a purpose in allowing evil to coexist with Him in this universe. It's hard to understand why. What we do know is that God has total authority in heaven and on the earth. God is sovereign over everything. Consequently, Satan has no authority to work in the life of a child of God without God's permission. Everything Satan is allowed to do is done within the permissive will of God.

Paul's words tell us that God permitted Satan to "buffet" Paul. "Buffet" is translated from the Greek word *kolaphizo*, which means "to strike with clenched hands . . . the fist."[4] This word implies constant, recurring attacks.

What is your response when trials and suffering come? How has it worked for you?

When God permits trials and suffering in our lives, we have several choices available to us.

We can blame God and become bitter. When we respond this way, it often hardens our hearts against God, preventing Him from being able to work in and through our circumstances. It pushes us farther and farther away from the very One who can help us.

We can surrender and give up in defeat. This response usually leads to despair, depression, and sometimes even hopelessness. It leads us to isolate ourselves from others and from God.

We can grit our teeth and suffer quietly to the bitter end. With this response, we use every ounce of our own strength to endure the trial. It leaves us drained and sapped of all energy. Because our strength alone is insufficient, we will eventually collapse physically, emotionally, and spiritually.

Paul's response is the better one. Paul didn't like his thorn. He didn't want it. He pleaded with God to take it away. I love this response because Paul gives us permission to tell God we don't like what He is doing and to please stop it! I hope this encourages you as much as it does me.

How many times did Paul ask God to take his thorn away?

Who else went before God three times asking Him to take something from Him? (Matthew 26:39–44)

Both the words of Jesus and of Paul teach us that praying repeatedly for God to change His plan doesn't reveal a lack of faith. Their stories give us permission to cry out to our Father for whatever burdens our hearts. God wants to know the cry of our hearts. In fact, He asks us to unload our burdens on Him so that He can carry them (Matthew 11:28–30).

Friend, God may not answer in the way we ask Him to, but the words and actions of both Jesus and Paul demonstrate that our unanswered prayer is not necessarily due to a lack of faith. Sometimes it is because God has another plan . . . a better plan.

Write God's answer to Paul below. (2 Corinthians 12:9a)

Despite Paul's desperate pleas, God did not take away his thorn. But He did give Paul a most amazing gift.

What was that gift?

Grace gives us what we do not deserve. Grace is God's provision for our every need when we need it.

God comforted Paul with these words: "My grace is sufficient" (2 Corinthians 9 NIV). "Sufficient" is translated from the Greek word *arkeo* and means "to be possessed of sufficient strength, to be *strong enough* for a thing." Friend, God's grace is always enough to sustain us. God's grace never runs dry. It is always enough! God tells us in His Word that He is the strength of our hearts and our portion forever (Psalm 73:26 NIV).

Not only is His grace sufficient; God adds this promise: "My power is made perfect in weakness." It is in our times of greatest weakness that God will pour out His power upon us. He created us in such a way that His power works most effectively when we are weak.

We cry out for God to take away that which burdens us and replace it with something else . . . health, healing, a job, finances, comfort, a baby, a husband. Sometimes God will do as we ask. But sometimes He won't because He has a transformational work to do in our lives. And the only way He can do His work, the only way He can bring us the blessing, is through the pain. Through His amazing grace, our affliction works *for* us and not *against* us.

Let's stop for a moment to meditate on what Paul has taught us. Prayerfully reread the passage for this day's lesson and any notes you have taken. Share in your own words what this passage is teaching you about the trials you are currently facing. How is God speaking to your heart to apply what you have learned?

As we end our lesson today, remember that God never explained Himself to Paul. He simply gave him a promise. *My grace is sufficient.* Friend, whenever you are walking through a trial, go to God's Word. Ask Him for a word. It's a must. It's where you will find a truth or a promise to speak into your circumstances. It's where you will find wisdom and discernment. It's where you will find hope.

God will speak to you. It's His promise. He speaks continually through His living and active Word. His Word is eternal and never changing. As you read it, study it. As you study it, memorize it. As you memorize it, pray it. It will come alive in you and transform you. So although your circumstances may not change, you will. Your perspective will change. Your heart will change. Your prayers will change. Your choices will change. Your witness and testimony will change.

God's grace transformed Paul's perspective, and it will transform yours.

Paul ended today's passage with these words:

Therefore I will boast all the more gladly about my weaknesses, *so that* Christ's power may rest on me. (2 Corinthians 12:9 NIV; emphasis added)

Paul says that he will boast about his weaknesses "so that" what?

Paul wanted more of Christ's power.

What does it look like to have Christ's power "rest" on us?

The word translated "rest" here means "to spread a tabernacle over." Don't you love this picture? We are frail creatures, created by God to need Him. He longs for us to admit our frailty and cry out for help so that He can come to our rescue. God is our covering . . . our Shield, our Defender, our Strength, and our Strong Tower.

Psalm 28:7 says, "The Eternal is the source of my strength and the shield that guards me. When I *learn to rest and* truly trust Him, He sends His help." His strength is sufficient to transform our weak, fragile bodies into glorious, holy tabernacles indwelt by His Spirit! First Corinthians 3:16 says, "Don't you know that you yourselves are God's temple and that God's Spirit lives in you?" (NIV).

As we close today, rejoice in God's promise: it is only when we are weak that we will be strong!

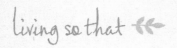
living so that

IF YOU WANT TO GO DEEPER:

Warren Wiersbe listed the following practical lessons to be learned from Paul's thorn:[5]

1. Spiritual blessings are more important than physical ones. Paul thought he could be a better Christian if God relieved him of his weakness, but just the opposite was true.

2. Unanswered prayer does not always mean the need is not met. Sometimes we receive a greater blessing when God does not answer our prayers. God always answers the need even though it seems He is not answering the prayer.

3. Weakness is strength if Christ is in it. (1 Corinthians 1:26–31)

4. There is grace to meet every need. Grace enabled Paul to accept his weakness, glory in it, and take pleasure in it. Paul knew that his weakness would bring glory to Christ, and that was enough for him. (2 Corinthians 4:7–10)

Read through these carefully. Does one speak to you? Spend time with that lesson, and ask God how you can bring it alive in your circumstances.

CONCLUDING THOUGHTS:

We focused our time on Paul's thorn in his side. Based on how God has spoken to your heart, complete the thought below.

Trials come so that . . .

PART THREE:
"That You May Believe"

MEMORY VERSE: CONSIDER IT PURE JOY, MY BROTHERS, WHENEVER YOU FACE TRIALS OF MANY KINDS, BECAUSE YOU KNOW THAT THE TESTING OF YOUR FAITH DEVELOPS PERSEVERANCE. PERSEVERANCE MUST FINISH ITS WORK **SO THAT** YOU MAY BE MATURE AND COMPLETE, NOT LACKING ANYTHING.

–James 1:2–4 (NIV; emphasis added)

God did not put us on this earth to live an easy, carefree life. We have a greater purpose here.

🖋 **Read Ephesians 2:10.** What does this say about why God created us?

God created each one of us to do good works in the kingdom of God. These are works He prepared in advance for us to do (Ephesians 2:10 NIV). Sometimes that preparation requires that we endure difficult trials. But in the trials, God makes two promises. First, our trials have purpose. Second, in the midst of them, He will never fail us or abandon us (Deuteronomy 31:6; Romans 8:38–39).

🖋 **Read Isaiah 45:2; 55:12.** What else does God promise?

God promises that He will go before us and behind us and lead us every step of the way.

🖋 **Read Romans 8:28.** What else does God promise?

Friend, *God promises that no matter the trial, no matter how impossible our circumstances may seem,* He will work all things together for good. Not some things, but *all* things. Not just the good things, but *all* things. "All" is inclusive.

It's important you understand that this text does not teach that bad things *are* good or that God makes bad things good. No, it teaches that God will use the bad things that happen in our lives to *bring about* good for His people.

"Together" translates the Greek word *sunergeo.* It is the word from which we get our word "synergism." Dr. David Jeremiah wrote, "Synergism is the working together of various elements to produce an effect greater than, and often completely different from, the sum of each element acting separately."[6]

God mixes together the many trials and tribulations through which we walk and causes them to work for good in our lives. So even though separately they might seem tragic and hopeless, as a whole, when combined with the power of the Holy Spirit, God harmonizes them for our ultimate good.

Did you notice that God's Romans 8:28 promise contains a condition?

🖋 What is the condition? Define those for whom God will work all things together for good.

If you are in the midst of a trial, I hope our lessons are teaching you that it is in God alone you will find hope. It is in Him you will find comfort and the strength to endure.

Read John 9:1–12.

This story opens with Jesus walking along and coming upon a man blind since birth. His disciples asked Him, "Teacher, who sinned? *Who is responsible for this man's blindness? Did he commit sins that merited this punishment? If not his sins, is it the sins of his parents?*" (John 9:2). They wanted to know the reason behind the man's blindness. But identifying the cause was not important to Jesus. He responded, "Neither. His blindness cannot be *explained or* traced to any particular person's sins. He is blind so the deeds of God may be put on display" (v. 3).

Why was this man born blind?

Does Jesus' answer bother you? If so, why?

For the Jews at that time, morality translated into a simple formula: those who lived in obedience to God were rewarded, and those who did not were punished. Consequently, they saw sickness, weakness, and personal failure as evidence of sin in a person's life (or in the life of his parents). Alternatively, they saw health, strength, and prosperity as evidence of God's favor. Sadly, there are many pastors and Bible teachers who continue to teach that message today.

It was this thinking that caused the disciples to ask Jesus, "Who sinned?"

🖋 What did Jesus answer?

Jesus answered definitively. He made it very clear that the man was born blind *so that* God could demonstrate His power through him. One Bible commentator described it this way: "[The blind man's] tragedy was a backdrop for a blessing!"[7]

I see this in my own story. After my attack, I asked God what I had done to deserve what happened to me that day in June. I felt abandoned by God. I locked myself in a prison of fear to protect myself. At times, daily living seemed too much to bear. Yet out of this trial grew a ministry. It is why you are reading these words today. God now uses my transformed life as a vessel to draw others to Him.

Sweet friend, my vicious assault serves as the backdrop for a precious teaching ministry He has given me. Could it be that the Lord wants to use the very trial you have suffered as a backdrop for a similar ministry?

The blind man's story reminds us that we are created for God's purposes alone, and the trials and sufferings that enter into our lives come to bring about the glory of God and point others to Him.

⤜ APPLICATION:

Today we find ourselves once again faced with choices in the midst of our messy lives. We can run toward God or away from God. When we run away from God, we will miss the lesson God wants us to learn. We will not experience the "good" that God is working in and through the trial. We will miss the blessings on the other side.

When we run toward God, we will find the lesson. We will experience the "good" and see God at work in our midst. We will receive the blessings on the other side.

God carefully placed stories throughout the pages of Scripture to show us He is ever present, ever working in our trials. These stories reveal that in times of prayer and waiting, studying and questioning, He is preparing us.

Let's move to the familiar story of Mary, Martha, and Lazarus.

Read John 11:1–45. What was the crisis? What did Mary and Martha do in response?

Lazarus was dying. Scripture does not reveal the cause of Lazarus's sickness, only that he was dying. Desperate and afraid of losing their brother, Mary and Martha sent an urgent message to Jesus.

How did Jesus respond? What was His reason? What is the "so that" here? (11:4 NIV)

Jesus received the message but did not come immediately. Despite His great love for Mary, Martha, and Lazarus, He intentionally stayed where He was two more days. When Jesus finally decided to take His disciples to visit Lazarus, he had already died.

🖋 What did Jesus say to His disciples when He announced it was time to go see Lazarus? (11:14–15 NIV)

🖋 What is the "so that" here?

Word of Jesus' arrival spread quickly. Martha ran out immediately and upon seeing Jesus said, "Lord, if You had been with us, my brother would not have died" (John 11:21).

🖋 With what words did Jesus reply to Martha? (11:25)

Jesus calmly replied with these words: "I am the resurrection and the source of all life" (John 11:25). He used two specific words, "resurrection" and "life," because He was preparing Martha.

Mary never did come out to see Jesus, so He sent for her. When Mary finally reached Jesus, she fell at His feet, weeping. Scripture says that as Jesus watched Mary collapse at His feet, He was deeply moved in spirit and wept. The Creator of the universe, the King of kings and Lord of lords, the Great I Am stood before the crowd of onlookers, tears leaking from His eyes. He knew what was about to happen; He knew He was about to raise Lazarus from the dead, yet He cried. Why? Jesus wept for their pain and grief. His tears revealed His great love for them. When we are in our place of pain and doubt, Jesus understands. He weeps with us. His friends' tears of grief were on His face! And, friend, so are yours.

Why did Jesus not answer the prayers of His beloved friends Mary and Martha? Can we trust a God who does this? Was this a game to Him? Before we can answer these questions accurately, we must read the rest of the story.

When Jesus arrived at the cave where Lazarus was buried, Jesus commanded those present to take away the stone.

Martha objected. Are we surprised?

Write the words Jesus spoke to Martha below. What did He mean? (11:40)

With that, they took away the stone. With every eye upon Him, Jesus boldly and loudly prayed to His Father in heaven:

> "Father, I am grateful that You have heard Me. I know that You are always listening, but I proclaim it loudly **so that** everyone here will believe You have sent Me." (John 11:41–42; bold emphasis added)

What is the "so that" here? What theme do you see in Jesus' words?

Then He called out in a loud voice, "Lazarus, come out!" (John 11:43). Out of the shadows of the cave emerged a mummy-like figure, a dead man bound with strips of linen. Jesus commanded, "Untie him, and let him go" (John 11:44).

At the command of Jesus, the One who told Martha He was the resurrection and the source of all life, a dead man came to life! Martha and Mary's brother was alive. Their prayers had been answered even more abundantly than they could have ever asked or imagined (see Ephesians 3:20).

John ends with these powerful words in John 11:45: "As a result, many of the Jews who had come with Mary saw what happened and believed in Him."

Why do I include this story? Because I want you to see what God does in the "wait." Mary and Martha were walking through their worst trial. They cried out to Jesus. They heard nothing. Jesus seemingly ignored their cries. Their brother died, and they still heard nothing. Can you imagine what they felt? They thought of Jesus as family. They thought He loved them. They knew He was able to heal. Yet He never came . . . never sent even a word.

When you doubt God, when you cannot understand what He is doing, or when you question whether He even hears your prayers, go to this story and others like it. Sit quietly. It is in this place that you will find the answers to your questions. These stories teach us that God never abandons His children, and He will never abandon you. Even when you cannot see Him, even when you cannot hear Him, even when you cannot feel Him, He is working in your midst.

Jesus is at work *so that* we will believe! He is at work *so that* glory and honor will come to His Father!

CONCLUDING THOUGHTS:

We focused our time today on a few stories from the gospel of John. Based on how God has spoken to your heart, complete the thought below.

Trials come so that . . .

PART FOUR:
Confident Faith to Endure

MEMORY VERSE: CONSIDER IT PURE JOY, MY BROTHERS,
WHENEVER YOU FACE TRIALS OF MANY KINDS, BECAUSE
YOU KNOW THAT THE TESTING OF YOUR FAITH DEVELOPS
PERSEVERANCE. PERSEVERANCE MUST FINISH ITS WORK **SO THAT**
YOU MAY BE MATURE AND COMPLETE, NOT LACKING ANYTHING.

–James 1:2-4 (NIV; emphasis added)

God desires that we not only trust Him in our trials but also walk confidently in them.

Read Hebrews 10:35–36.

> So do not throw away your confidence; it will be richly rewarded.
> You need to persevere *so that* when you have done the will of God,
> you will receive what he has promised. (NIV; emphasis added)

The circumstances surrounding our trials sometimes make it so easy to throw away our confidence. Maybe it's a time when nothing is going as planned. Maybe it's a time of unanswered prayer. Maybe it's a time when we cannot see, feel, or hear God. Maybe it's a time of physical weariness or chronic sickness. The reasons are many and varied. We all have them, times we want to give up and walk away.

What we forget during those times is that we have full access to God's power and His promises. It is in that power and those promises that we will find our confidence. This is not the world's confidence. It is Christ's confidence. Is there a difference? Absolutely.

The world's confidence is based on what we see with our eyes and what we feel with our emotions. Christ's confidence is based on Christ and who He is. We don't gain Christ's confidence by simply asking for it. *We have to take action.*

My friend Renee Swope, author of *A Confident Heart*, advises that if we find ourselves in this situation we must do two things. First, when feelings of doubt and uncertainty arise, we must immediately stop and ask God to help us identify what is causing our doubt and uncertainty. Second, after we identify the cause of our doubt, we must compare our thoughts about our situation with God's thoughts, which are found in His Word.

Do they match? If they do, then we must meditate on and pray through those truths, holding fast to them and trusting God to use them to carry us through. Scripture clearly teaches in Isaiah 55:11 that God honors His Word and that His Word will not return empty but will accomplish what He desires and achieve the purposes for which He sends it (NIV).

If they don't match, we must search His Word for truths and promises to replace the lies we are hearing and often believing.[8] We find this truth in 2 Corinthians 10:5, which says we are to "demolish arguments and every pretension that sets itself up against the knowledge of God, and . . . take captive every thought to make it obedient to Christ" (NIV).

⋙ APPLICATION:

A few years ago, we dropped our daughter off at the University of Georgia for her freshman year of college. Athens, Georgia, is about three hours from our house. Every time Lauren got in her car to make the return trip to Athens after a visit home, I would pray with and for her. Each time she drove away, tears would fall, and I would beg God to carry her safely back to school. I prayed specifically for no mechanical difficulties.

On one of those trips, we received a call about an hour after her departure. Her voice was shaky, and she was trying hard to hold back tears. She spoke words no parent of a teenage daughter wants to hear: "I have a flat tire." Upon hearing those words, I quickly handed the phone to her daddy. When she got on the phone with him, Lauren broke down, sobbing. She was fearful because it was dusk, and she was alone on the side of the road, with no one to help her. Although Monty had taught her how to change a tire, she was in no shape to take on that monumental task. She was nervous and afraid.

I must confess that, as a Bible teacher, I did not model what I teach. I did not "walk my talk." As I listened to my husband calm her, I began to cry. As time passed, I grew frantic and could not control my emotions. Fear gripped me as it had not done in years. I pictured my sweet baby girl terrified, alone, sitting in her car, crying. I pictured a man pulling up behind her, walking to her car, feigning help, and then kidnapping her. Every thought that came to me was a complete lie from the evil one, but I allowed those thoughts access and I replayed them in my head.

The one wise decision I made was to call a few friends to pray. But did *I* pray? No, I worried. Prayer was impossible at the time because I had allowed my emotions to take over.

Thank goodness for my husband, who reacted reasonably and rationally. He called AAA. Lauren was not on our membership. At first, the woman told my husband that they could not send help for her since she was not listed on our membership, and we were not present with her. But God . . . ! When the woman learned of Lauren's circumstances and that she was eighteen and alone on the side of the road, she not only allowed Lauren to use our membership but also called the highway patrol so they would send a car Lauren's way to ensure her safety.

What I struggled with the most was the fact that I had specifically prayed for this *not* to happen.

God does not always give us what we pray. Sometimes trouble, sickness, and tragedy will come. Sometimes God does not intervene and allows the trial. Why?

Throughout these lessons, we have studied many reasons why. One we have not discussed is *who* God is.

Read Isaiah 46:8–11. What truths about God do you glean from this passage?

Friend, God knows how to run the universe, the world, and even our lives better than we do. He is omnipotent, meaning He is all-powerful. Nothing happens outside His sovereign hand.

Read the words of this old familiar hymn, "A Firm Foundation":

How firm a foundation, ye saints of the Lord,
Is laid for your faith in His excellent word!
What more can He say than to you He hath said—
To you who for refuge to Jesus have fled?

"Fear not, I am with thee, oh, be not dismayed,
For I am thy God, and will still give thee aid;
I'll strengthen thee, help thee, and cause thee to stand,
Upheld by My gracious, omnipotent hand.

"When through the deep waters I call thee to go,
The rivers of sorrow shall not overflow;
For I will be with thee thy trouble to bless,
And sanctify to thee thy deepest distress.

"When through fiery trials thy pathway shall lie,
My grace, all-sufficient, shall be thy supply;
The flame shall not harm thee; I only design
Thy dross to consume and thy gold to refine.

"The soul that on Jesus doth lean for repose,
I will not, I will not, desert to his foes;
That soul, though all hell should endeavor to shake,
I'll never, no never, no never forsake."

Read through this hymn and point out the spiritual truths that speak to God's role in our trials and suffering.*

Choose a few words or phrases that spoke to you; look them up in the concordance in the back of your Bible. If you don't have a concordance, visit www.biblegateway.com, place your words in the "Keyword Search" box, and note the scriptures you find. Write these down in your Bible or in a special place where you can access them when you need them.

It isn't that we cannot have a time of panic when difficult news comes our way. The key is to not stay in panic mode. We must *stop* and examine our response. If we are not responding in faith, we must identify our response and change it immediately.

What does it look like to respond in faith? Certainly not my response!

Faith asks these questions:

1. What is God trying to teach me?

2. Am I claiming God's promises and truths?

3. Am I disobeying God?

---

* For example, what touched my heart was "the rivers of sorrow shall not overflow." Those words led me to Isaiah 43:2, "When you pass through the waters, I will be with you; and when you pass through the rivers, they will not sweep over you" (NIV).

4. Am I harboring unforgiveness?

5. Am I humbling my heart to see if there is any way in me that displeases God?

6. Am I trusting God that no matter how my trial turns out, I will give Him all glory and honor and praise?

Are you currently walking through a trial? Are you suffering and cannot see God in the midst? Sit before the Lord with the verses you have found, the questions listed, and the truths you have learned. Invite Him to speak and move in your midst and to show you His glory. Journal below what you hear. Write a prayer.

As we close today, I want to leave you with this thought: in every trial that I've brought before the Lord, He has faithfully met me in one place . . . His Word. Yes, there are times He has spoken through a friend, a pastor, or even a worship song. But when I have sought Him in His Word, never once has He failed me. The only failure has come when I've gone my own way and not turned to Him. He alone is faithful and true.

George Mueller, at the age of ninety, was quoted as saying that he had never experienced unanswered prayer. Below are two quotes from this mighty man of God:

> I always pray with an open Bible, filling my praise and petition with God's word. I pray God's promises, His declarations concerning Himself. I pray His name and titles by which He reveals His nature and character. I pray the rights He gave the believer to bold and confident access. When a need arose, I spread them all out before God who hears His children. My heavenly Father will not break His word to His own child.[9]

The Lord gives faith, for the very purpose of trying it for the glory of His own name, and for the good of him who has it; and, by the very trial of our faith, we not only obtain blessing to our own souls, by becoming the better acquainted with God, if we hold fast our confidence in Him, but our faith is also, by the exercise, strengthened: and so it comes, that, if we walk with God in any measure of uprightness of heart, the trials of faith will be greater and greater.[10]

One of my favorite "so that" verses is found in the Old Testament. **Read Joshua 1:7–9.** This is God's charge to Joshua, His chosen replacement for Moses. List God's commands to Joshua.

God was not saying that Joshua wouldn't have trials, because they materialized in the very next chapter. But God was promising that He would be with Joshua through those trials and that Joshua would come out victorious in the end.

A barometer is an instrument that measures atmospheric pressure, the weight of the air in the atmosphere. If the weight of mercury is less than the atmospheric pressure, the mercury level in the glass tube rises. If the weight of mercury is more than the atmospheric pressure, the mercury level falls. Friend, how we handle adversity is an accurate barometer of where we are spiritually. When our barometer gives a low reading, it may be because we do not have an accurate understanding of God or because we do not have a strong foundation in His Word. And sometimes the way God chooses to increase our barometer reading is through trials. Trials are often the only thing that will drive us to our knees.

You should greatly rejoice *in what is waiting for you*, even if now for a little while you have to suffer various trials. *Suffering tests your faith which is more valuable than gold* (remember that gold, although it is perishable, is tested by fire) **so that** if it is found genuine, you can receive praise, honor, and glory when Jesus the Anointed, *our Liberating King,* is revealed at last. (1 Peter 1:6–7; bold emphasis added)

Yes, our faith is precious, but the trials of our faith are also precious because it is in and through them that we grow closer to God. Can there be any better place?

🢡🢡 IF YOU WANT TO GO DEEPER:

🖋 Read Nehemiah 4:1–20.

When God's people returned to their land after being in exile, they found their city defenseless, the wall around Jerusalem broken and its gates burned. After months of prayer and fasting, Nehemiah approached the king for permission to rebuild the wall. God granted Nehemiah favor with the king, and he gave permission to rebuild the wall. The Jews were elated. But opposition arose. Israel's enemies banded together and began to ridicule the Jews because they did not want the wall rebuilt. Day and night they taunted the Jews. They mocked them and accused them of rebelling against the king.

🖋 How did Nehemiah respond? (v. 4)

Rather than take action against his opponents, Nehemiah prayed and called on God to fight for him. Nehemiah knew that the Lord heard the sneers and the taunts. He knew God was his Defender. Nehemiah had only one concern, and that was for the glory of God. He did not want victory for himself but for God's people.

Nehemiah's response provides a great model for us. Persecution, false accusations, rejection, and/or betrayal may hurt, but they don't have to destroy us. We have a choice. It's up to us whether or not we allow the words and actions of others to take root in our hearts and minds. Satan will relentlessly pursue us with doubts, fear, anxiety, and other ungodly thoughts. But God, our Defender, provides the way out. Once again, we find that way out in the Word of God in what should be a familiar verse by now.

Let's revisit 2 Corinthians 10:5.

Read 2 Corinthians 10:5 and write it below.

The key, my friend, is to *identify* the lie and *replace* it with a truth. And then pray . . . pray . . . pray.

Nehemiah's enemies wanted nothing more than to distract him and eventually halt the building of the wall. But Nehemiah knew that, so again, he _____ .

What did Nehemiah pray?

The Jews continued rebuilding the wall, but this only heightened the enemies' anger. They plotted together to come against Jerusalem and fight.

✒ What was Nehemiah's response in verse 9?

Nehemiah did more than just pray this time. He combined faith with action. What a great example for us, because we, too, are in a battle. Our battle is not against flesh and blood but against Satan and his demonic forces, who use flesh and blood to discourage and come against us. Remember Ephesians 6:18 told us to "be alert" (NIV). We must be alert and watch for the evil one's handiwork in our midst. If we focus only on the *visible* enemy and forget the *invisible* enemy, we risk trusting our own resources, rather than God's. God's resources—the Word and prayer—are what enable us to recognize Satan's schemes and his lies.

✒ What happened in verses 10–12?

Discouragement will come in any spiritual battle, my friend. It's one of Satan's favorite weapons. It is the one that convinces us to raise the white flag and give up. We must be armed and prepared to fight through the discouragement and despair. We must have a foundation upon which to stand and a weapon with which to defend.

Nehemiah did just that in verses 13–14.

What did Nehemiah do in verse 13? How does Mark 13:32–37 reinforce Nehemiah's actions?

Nehemiah stationed people at the weakest points in the wall, at the exposed places. He posted them by family and armed them. Each family held tools *and* weapons so they could both work and fight. Their goal: to finish the work no matter the cost. They kept working, yet they were prepared for battle.

What did Nehemiah encourage the people to do in verse 14? Write Nehemiah's words in verse 20 in the space below.

The more we obsess over the enemy's attacks, the more he will gain a foothold in our circumstances, and eventually in our hearts and in our homes. We must cut him off at his knees. Like Nehemiah, we must pray and commit our circumstances to the Lord, and then *get back to our work*! Anything that keeps us from doing that which God has called us to do will only aid the enemy.

CONCLUDING THOUGHTS:

Based on how God has spoken to your heart, complete the thought below.

Trials come so that . . .

PART FIVE:
The God of All Comfort

MEMORY VERSE: CONSIDER IT PURE JOY, MY BROTHERS,
WHENEVER YOU FACE TRIALS OF MANY KINDS, BECAUSE
YOU KNOW THAT THE TESTING OF YOUR FAITH DEVELOPS
PERSEVERANCE. PERSEVERANCE MUST FINISH ITS WORK **SO THAT**
YOU MAY BE MATURE AND COMPLETE, NOT LACKING ANYTHING.

—James 1:2–4 (NIV; emphasis added)

A great paradox of the Christian faith is that we experience God the most not in the best of times, but in the worst of times. As I have walked through trials, I've learned that when I turned *to* God, rather than *away* from God, the trial has strengthened my faith and drawn me closer to Him. Why? Because it is in trials that we most experience God's comfort and His presence.

Scripture teaches us that God is the Father of compassion and the God of all comfort.

Read 2 Corinthians 1:3–5.

All praise goes to God, Father of our Lord Jesus, the Anointed One. He is the Father of compassion, the God of all comfort. He consoles us as we endure the pain and hardship of life **so that** we may draw from His comfort and share it with others in their own struggles. For even as His suffering continues to flood over us, through the Anointed we experience the wealth of His comfort just the same. (Bold emphasis added)

APPLICATION:

The NIV rendering of this passage gives praise to the God "who comforts us in all our troubles." How reassuring it is to know that we have a God who promises to comfort us in our troubles. And He doesn't just comfort us in some troubles; His Word says He comforts us in "all our troubles." The word "trouble" is a translation of the Greek word *thlipsis*. Etymologically (having to do with the origin of the word) it meant "to squeeze or crush," like processing grapes or crushing wheat to make flour. Figuratively, it came to be used to describe physical or emotional suffering. The Greek word means "a pressing, pressure . . . anything that burdens the spirit." William Barclay quotes a nineteenth-century archbishop who wrote, "When, according to the ancient law of England, those who willfully refused to plead had heavy weights placed on their breasts, and were so pressed and crushed to death, this was literally *thlipsis*."[11] The archbishop's description gives us a powerful visual for the word Paul chose to use here.

Suffering has been a part of the Christian life for centuries. Followers of Jesus suffered great persecution. Family and friends often shunned them. They endured relentless hostility from their pagan neighbors and the Roman government.

Paul himself endured incessant persecution. He knew what it meant to suffer. But the good news he shares is that in his suffering, he experienced God's comfort.

Paul identifies God as "God, Father of our Lord Jesus, the Anointed One. He is the Father of _____ , the God of all _____ ."

How many times does Paul use the word "comfort" in these three verses?

"Comfort" is a translation of the Greek word *paraklesis*, which means "a calling to one's side." This same word is used in John 14–16 for the Holy Spirit. It means much more than God sympathizing with us. It is God actually coming alongside us and ministering to us.

What do you do and/or where do you go when you are hurt, discouraged, or afraid?

When I'm discouraged, it's so easy for me to sink into my emotions and remain there, soaking in self-pity. I replay the hurt, the choices made, and the words spoken. I forget to go first to the One who can really comfort me . . . the only One who truly knows me.

Read Psalm 139:1–16. Share how this passage speaks to what we are talking about in this lesson.

God sent His Holy Spirit to be our Comforter so that He could minister to us during these times. And the Spirit's comfort is not a spiritual pacifier or a quick-fix pat on the shoulder. God's Holy Spirit gives us an infusion of strength that enables us to not only withstand our circumstances but also claim victory on the other side.

The psalmist speaks of the One who helps us in Psalm 121:1–2:

> I lift up my eyes to the hills—
> Where does my help come from?

My help comes from the LORD,
The Maker of heaven and earth. (NIV)

Have you had a time in your life when you have felt the Holy Spirit's comfort? In what form did He bring it?

Read 2 Corinthians 1:4. What is the "so that" in this verse? God comforts us "so that" what?

In verse 4, Paul gives another reason for our suffering. God comforts us in our troubles *so that* we can share the comfort we have received with others. Paul specifically wrote that we can comfort those in *any* trouble with the comfort we received. What this means is that even when another's pain and suffering may be different from ours, it does not affect our ability to minister to that friend. We can still comfort him or her with the same comfort we received.

What a beautiful thought. You and I are God's vessels of comfort. When God appears absent and distant to a friend, we are the one whom our friend can see, hear, feel, and touch.

Doctors diagnosed our daughter, Lauren, with progressing scoliosis in seventh grade. Initially, we tried to correct it without surgery. She wore a brace for nearly nine months. When this did not arrest the movement of the spine, we turned to chiropractic care. This course of treatment worked well until Lauren experienced a huge growth spurt. At that point, nothing worked to stop the aggressive curvature of her spine. Finally, during her junior year of high school, the curvature reached a point where surgery became necessary.

It was a long, trying journey. I will never forget the tears my sweet girl cried the first time she looked in the mirror and saw herself in the back brace she had to wear twenty-three hours a day, seven days a week. I will never forget when we told her she had to give up competitive cheerleading. I will never forget the excruciating pain and discomfort she endured as she underwent painful chiropractic adjustments four days a week. I will never forget the agonizing seven and a half hours my husband and I sat in the family waiting room, hoping and praying for word of a successful surgery. And I will never forget standing by her hospital bed as she writhed in pain, pleading with us to press the pain pump to receive more morphine.

How could this ever have any good purpose?

But it did. Through this journey, Lauren discovered that she was a strong and courageous young woman. Her faith grew by leaps and bounds. As a family, we saw glimpses of God at work nearly every day. We experienced the God of all comfort in all His fullness.

Since that day, God has allowed Lauren and me to walk alongside other moms and daughters who have made this same journey. We have prayed with them, shared wisdom and advice, and given warnings and encouragement—and Lauren even created a "words of wisdom and advice" booklet for girls going through her surgery.

God worked all things, even this heartbreaking diagnosis, together for His good. God used Lauren's experience to enable us to be a very real source of comfort and encouragement to others.

Vulnerability is the key, my friend. We must be willing to reveal our frailties and our pain so that others can see what God has done in us. It doesn't seem to make sense, but when we allow others to see our weakness, that's when we display God's strength the most!

God created us to live in community, and within that community, to love and serve one another. Beginning with Jesus and His disciples and continuing through the book of Acts, God placed His people in small groups to devote themselves to teaching, fellowship, breaking bread together, and praying (Acts 2:42). He never intended for us to live alone or suffer alone. We are to live and suffer together.

IF YOU WANT TO GO DEEPER:

Let's end today with 1 Corinthians 10:13.

> Any temptation you face will be nothing new. But God is faithful, and He will not let you be tempted beyond what you can handle. But He always provides a way of escape **so that** you will be able to endure *and keep moving forward*. (Bold emphasis added)

What truths do you learn about temptation in this verse?

As long as we live in this world, we will not escape temptation because we have an enemy of our soul who "is prowling around . . . like a roaring lion, just waiting *and hoping for the chance* to devour someone" (1 Peter 5:8). And we will never be free of temptation because the source of temptation lives within us . . . our flesh. Our flesh is weak. We give in to temptation when we don't have the tools to combat it.

Being in the Word is essential to overcoming temptation. Scripture reveals Satan's lies. It keeps us alert to his schemes. If we are not in the Word and not alert, temptation creeps in. Little by little, it causes us to make little compromises. The more compromises we make, the easier it becomes to give in, until the temptation finally overtakes us.

If we compromise long enough, we reach something that John of the Cross, sixteenth-century monk and great devotion writer, called "the dark night of the soul." We enter into a time of darkness and hopelessness. The pleasure we once experienced in our relationship with God dissipates. Feelings of joy and delight vanish. We feel alone. God feels distant. We no longer hear His voice. We no longer sense His presence.

God uses this "dark night" as a purifying place.

King David went through several dark nights of the soul. Following one such occasion, he wrote Psalm 32 as a grateful testimony for God's gift of forgiveness.

Read Psalm 32. Share what you learn from David in this psalm.

Read Psalm 42. How does the psalmist describe himself? (vv. 1–3, 9) What does the psalmist ask, and what is his answer? (vv. 5–6, 11)

Have you ever experienced what might be called a "dark night" in your spiritual journey? Describe what brought you to that place and how you felt.

How do we return from a dark night of the soul?

John of the Cross wrote:

Let's suffice to say, then, that God perceives the imperfections within us, and because of his love for us, urges us to grow up. His love is not content to leave us in our weakness, and for this reason he takes us into a dark night. He weans us from all of the pleasures by giving us dry times and inward darkness. In doing so he is able to take away all these vices and create virtues within us . . . No soul will ever grow deep in the spiritual life unless God works passively in that soul by means of a dark night.[12]

Share your thoughts on his words.

Do you see, my friend, that on the other side of the dark night of the soul we find a deeper, richer relationship with God? If you find yourself in a dark night right now, hang on with all your might. God is with you. He is in your dark night. He will not leave you or forsake you. He will work this time for His good. Trust Him.

CONCLUDING THOUGHTS:

Every year on June 7, the anniversary of my attack, something deep within me triggered a sense of sorrow and grief. It's as if deep within, my body remembered the extreme violation it endured that day. Several years ago, twenty years after my attack, having just returned from working out at the Y, I jumped into the shower. For some crazy reason, as I stepped out of the shower, I recalled the date. It was June 8. The anniversary of my rape had passed. After twenty years of memorializing that as a day of mourning and sadness, it had not even crossed my memory. Joy and praise erupted from my lips. God's promise fulfilled . . . the old had gone and the new had come.

A few days later in my quiet time, God placed Psalm 40 in front of me. It was not a psalm with which I was familiar. He impressed these words on my heart just before I read it: *This is your life, sweet child. This is why I allowed so many years of pain and suffering in your life.* I then read these words:

> I waited patiently for the LORD; he turned to me and heard my cry. He lifted me out of the slimy pit, out of the mud and mire; he set my feet on a rock and gave me a firm place to stand. He put a new song in my mouth, a hymn of praise to our God. Many will see and fear and put their trust in the LORD. (Psalm 40:1–3 NIV)

Every word of this passage reflected my journey. On the other side of this "dark night of the soul," God gave me a passionate love for His Word and a giftedness to teach it. He gave me a ministry and a calling. God worked this horrific tragedy in my life for good because I loved Him and was called according to His purpose!

⇒》 MY CALL TO ACTION:

What have you heard from the Lord this week? What steps is He asking you to take regarding a trial in your life? Commit now to take the first steps in obedience to what you have heard. Journal and pray in the space below.

CHAPTER FIVE

Let Your Light Shine So That...

MEMORY VERSE: YOU ARE THE LIGHT OF THE WORLD . . . LET YOUR LIGHT SHINE BEFORE MEN, **[SO] THAT** THEY MAY SEE YOUR GOOD DEEDS AND PRAISE YOUR FATHER IN HEAVEN.

—Matthew 5:14, 16 (NIV; emphasis added)

PRAYER:

Heavenly Father, thank You for Your faithfulness to walk with me through these lessons. You have poured truth into my heart and mind. You have given me a spirit of knowledge and revelation to understand Your Word and apply it in my life. You have convicted and refined me. I am so thankful for this precious time in Your Word. Lead me to my next steps with You. Give me a hunger and thirst for more of You. Open doors for me to live out what I have learned. I want to live a "so that" life. Give me the courage to obey my Calls to Action. Use me, Lord, to make a difference in Your kingdom. Instruct me daily in the way I should go. Keep my eyes fixed on You. Give me opportunities to share the hope I have in You and to share the truth and promises found in Your living and active Word. I love You, Lord, and ask all this in Jesus' name. Amen.

PART ONE:
⇛ Be Transformed

She walked among us on campus every day. Her blonde hair, confident stature, and winning smile drew everyone's attention. But beyond the physical beauty, something about her captivated us. Maybe it was the unspoken joy; the sweetness of her spirit; the lack of grumbling and complaining; or maybe that a cross word never came from her lips. If you ever needed a word of encouragement, Lendy was your girl. I had never met anyone quite like her. I always wondered, *What does she have that I don't?*

Over time, we became friends. I thought eventually I would see another side to her . . . the side that was more like me. But still she never uttered a word of complaint or morsel of gossip. She would always find the best in every person and circumstance. It was crazy!

As we grew closer, I learned her secret. It was her faith. Her faith was different from mine. I grew up in the Catholic Church. My parents took me to church regularly. I attended catechism classes. I prayed sometimes and read the Bible now and again. Others I knew had a Baptist or a Lutheran faith. But Lendy's faith was not rooted in the church she attended. Rather, it was rooted in what she called her "relationship" with Jesus. I didn't understand what she meant at the time. But one thing I knew is that I wanted to understand. I wanted some of what she had.

> *Lendy's faith was not rooted in the church she attended. Rather, it was rooted in what she called her "relationship" with Jesus.*

John uses the concept of *koinonia* to describe this special relationship Lendy had with Jesus. First John 1:3 says, "We proclaim to you what we have seen and heard, *so that* you also may have fellowship with us. And our fellowship is with the Father and with his Son, Jesus Christ" (NIV; emphasis added).

Koinonia is a word of intimacy and means "partnership, partakers; participation." The Amplified Bible translation more richly describes this relationship in 1 John 1:3:

> What we have seen and [ourselves] heard, we are also telling you, so that you too may realize and enjoy fellowship as partners and partakers with us. And [this] fellowship that we have [*which is a distinguishing mark of Christians*] is with the Father and with His Son Jesus Christ (the Messiah). (Emphasis added)

And what a distinguishing mark it was in her life!

What the words of both Matthew and John reveal is their desire for us to know this same kind of fellowship: a warm, comfortable relationship with God in which we are connected to Him in heart and mind and living that out and sharing it with others.

What was the difference between my friend and me? We were both Christians. But I blended into my world. I fit in with everyone else, acting and living just as they did. She did not. She stood out. She shone Christ's light on everyone around her.

In this chapter, we will examine different ways we can shine our light and make a difference in our world.

➤➤ APPLICATION:

Jesus said, "I am the light of the world" (John 8:12 NIV). Why did He call Himself "light"? Remember: Jesus came to earth not only to redeem us but also to reveal God to man. Just before this declaration, Jesus had exposed the sin of the scribes and Pharisees who brought the woman guilty of adultery before Him to see how she should be punished. When He pointed out their sin and showed them they were just as guilty as she, they fled. They thought their sin was hidden. But nothing is hidden from the eyes of God.

We do not have Jesus physically in our midst, so how do we experience the "Light of the world" today?

Read the following passages to answer this question. Share what you find.

1. Psalm 19:7–11

2. Psalm 119:105

3. Psalm 119:130

4. Proverbs 2:1–6

5. Proverbs 6:23

How has the Word of God been a source of light in your life? Have you noticed a connection between darkness/times of sin and your time in the Word?

There is a dark side to this world. It invades our lives daily when we connect to the outside world through the Internet, our favorite morning show, or the newspaper. A mother has drowned her children. A college coed has been brutally raped and murdered. An innocent child has been abducted by a convicted child molester out on parole. A mentally ill man has walked into a quiet neighborhood movie theater and brutally slain innocent men, women, and children. Some days I find myself praying for Jesus' return.

But there is a dark side within us too. Paul expressed it well in Romans 7:19 when he wrote, "I can determine that I am going to do good, but I don't do it; instead, I end up living out the evil that I decided not to do."

God is our only hope in the midst of this darkness. He promises that He will never fail or abandon us (Deuteronomy 31:6; Romans 8:38–39)! God is light, and in Him there is no darkness at all (1 John 1:5 NKJV). He is holy, good, and pure.

To live in the light means being real with God. It requires surrender, confession, repentance, and obedience. We must continually expose our hearts and minds to His Word. While there, we must allow Him to teach us new ways to think and act.

So, before we dig in, take a few minutes and sit with God. Invite Him to reveal any darkness lurking in your heart, a hidden sin you are afraid to confess. We cannot have *koinonia* with God if we harbor this kind of sin in our hearts. God wants nothing more than to free us from places of darkness. He is waiting to forgive . . . to remove that sin as far as the east is from the west! Don't let Satan keep you trapped in a place of darkness. Accept your Father's forgiveness and come out into the light.

When we step out of darkness and into His light, God calls us to do more than bask in the Son's light. We are to shine the light and love of Christ within us to this dark and broken world. Luke 8:16 says:

> You wouldn't light a lamp and cover it with a clay pot. You're not going to hide it under your bed. No, when you light it, you're going to put it out in the open so your guests *can feel welcome and see where they're going.*

Our response to God's truth is a great indicator of our relationship with Him. Those who know Jesus most intimately are those who hear God's Word and put it into practice (Luke 8:21). We are not given the secrets of the kingdom of God to hoard them. We are given them to live out and to share.

Friend, I hope you are coming to understand what a great privilege it is to hear and understand the Word of God. God has entrusted us with a great treasure and commands us to share that treasure with others. When we receive the Word, God calls us to become sowers of the seed, bearers of His light, and voices for His truth. In fact, Luke ends this section warning us that if we keep what we have learned to ourselves, we will lose it; but if we share it, we will receive more.

John goes even further. He says in 1 John 1:4, "Retelling this story fulfills our joy." What John is saying is that by proclaiming the gospel and living in fellowship with those who hear and respond, his joy is fulfilled. When we as believers don't hoard what we learn but share it with our sphere of influence, we retain our true fellowship with God and one another. In doing this, we, like John, will experience true joy. *Koinonia* makes our joy fulfilled.

I am praying for you today, sweet friend: may your joy be fulfilled!

Letting our light shine before men does not come naturally. It requires a new way of thinking and acting. It means bringing our thoughts and actions in line with God's Word; it means living out what we have learned for the world to see.

Romans 12:2 says, "Do not conform any longer to the pattern of this world, but be transformed by the renewing of your mind. *Then* you will be able to test and approve what God's will is—his good, pleasing and perfect will" (NIV; emphasis added).

The Voice says it this way:

> Do not allow this world to mold you in its own image. Instead, be transformed *from the inside out* by renewing your mind. As a result, you will be able to discern what God wills and whatever God finds good, pleasing, and complete.

What is the "pattern of this world" to which Paul refers in Romans 12:2 (NIV)?

🖋 List some ways the world "molds" us into its image.

🖋 What are some ways you feel you are being molded into the world's image?

Conform, as used here, means "to fashion or shape one thing like another." Paul warned his audience, "Do not conform your lives to the present age in which you live." Conformists fear being different and long to be like—and liked by—everyone. They are followers because they do not want to miss anything or be left out.

I'm going to share a story with you, one I am not proud of, but that I feel I need to share to get my point across here. On my sixteenth birthday, I hosted a party at my house. My best friend and I invited a group of girls over to celebrate. We were both army brats and attended this great private school in our town. It was hard to fit in at first, but we finally had! We'd made it to the "in" crowd. When we invited the girls, we told them to wear pink shirts. However, we intentionally did not share our plan with one particular girl. She, too, was an army brat, but she was shy and struggled more to fit in.

The "popular" girls arrived one by one in their pink shirts. When Julie (I have changed her name) arrived in a different-colored shirt, it was so painfully obvious what we had done. (This could have been a scene from the movie *Mean Girls*!) Initially, we had hidden our cruel scheme from my parents. But when they saw the expression on Julie's face, I got one of "those" looks from my mom.

At the time, I had no idea the hurt I had caused my supposed friend because I was so wrapped up in myself and my cohorts. But I look back now, and it breaks my heart that we plotted such a heartless act. We make such terrible decisions when we desperately want to "fit in." I am truly ashamed.

How callous we can be when we conform to this world. We say yes to things when we know we should say no. We engage in conversations that tear others down rather than build them up. We watch television shows and movies that we know are displeasing to the Lord. Eventually, we become so accustomed to the world's ways that we think they're acceptable, the norm.

Paul taught that, rather than conform, we are to be "transformed" by the renewing of our minds. The Greek verb translated "transformed" is *metamorphoo.* We see it in the English word "metamorphosis," a biological change whereby a caterpillar becomes a butterfly. This is such a perfect picture of transformation. One creature enters the cocoon and a totally different creature emerges . . . a much more beautiful creature. Metamorphosis results in a total change from the inside out. For believers, the key to this transformation is our minds.

If the Holy Spirit is to have control over us, He must control our minds as well as our hearts.

"Mind" here is a translation of the Greek word *nous.* It denotes the part of our mind necessary for making decisions. Basically, it is the control center for perceiving and understanding, feeling and judging. If the Holy Spirit is to have control over us, He must control our minds as well as our hearts. This is why Paul calls us to continually renew our minds.

🖋 List ways we can renew our minds. (See Psalm 119:9–11; Philippians 2:5–7, 14–16; 4:6–9; Colossians 3:1–2; James 1:19–25; 3:13–17.)

Renewing our minds brings life transformation. We trade the "pattern of this world" (NIV) for kingdom values. We begin to put others' needs before our own. We seek to please Christ and not ourselves.

Life transformation prompts "so that" living.

Let me say that one more time. Life transformation prompts "so that" living.

To bring this truth alive, I want to share a story with you. Some friends and I began a neighborhood Bible study made up of typical suburban moms. We were all about the same age, with similar backgrounds, and all had young children.

One day a new woman moved into our neighborhood. I knew in my heart I should invite her to join our Bible study. But she made me a bit uncomfortable, so I didn't. Suzanne (not her real name) did not "fit in" with my world. She had piercings covering her body (nose, tongue, belly, etc.) and tattoos everywhere. She lived a life many Christians might characterize as self-indulgent and ungodly; she partied, drank too much, and often left her children unsupervised and out of control.

Over the next year, God put Suzanne across my path several times. I was always polite but never really engaged in conversation. Following each encounter, I left with an ache in my heart, knowing God was calling me to more, but doing nothing.

One evening, unbeknownst to me, Suzanne came to an event at my church during which I shared my testimony. After I spoke, women gathered at the front for prayer. I looked over and could not believe my eyes. In the sea of faces, I saw Suzanne, tears streaming down her face. As I approached her to offer a comforting hug, she cried softly into my ear, "I want what you have!" She saw something she hungered for . . . something different, something hopeful, something good. She wept and wept from the depths of her soul. In that moment, compassion poured forth, and I held her.

Did I follow up? She lived down the street from me, for heaven's sake! No, I did not. But God never gives up when He has a plan. Suzanne was seeking. And our God promises that when we seek Him with all our hearts, we will find Him (Jeremiah 29:13–14 NIV). Suzanne was seeking, and I was one of the women He had chosen to help point her to Him.

A few months later, He put her across my path again. She was pregnant with her third child—don't think my judgmental heart did not begin to judge that choice. She asked if we could talk. She shared her story. The rawness of her pain and sorrow pierced my soul.

> Our God promises that when we seek Him with all our hearts, we will find Him.

Suzanne had spent the last few years of her life filling the emptiness she had described with alcohol, drinking to numb her pain. For a time, she said, the emptiness would dissipate, but it always returned. She confessed how over the years, she had tried to fill that empty place with many things.

God gave me the words to respond. I told her that the "empty place" she kept referring to was a place in her heart created by God. It was a place that only He could fill. I shared with her that nothing else in this world would ever satisfy the craving that she felt. She hungered for more, so finally I invited her to our Bible study (I'm sure God was saying, "It's about time, Wendy!"). Another friend of mine and I took her a Bible to ensure she would have one the first day of study.

In just a few short months, God transformed Suzanne's life from the inside out. She dug into her homework. She would invest time over and above the assigned work, sometimes spending hours in the Word. She was hungry for truth, and God was faithful to give it. She grew to know she was loved unconditionally, freely forgiven, and valued as a child of God. I can't think of a better way to show you her heart than to include this excerpt from a part of our homework. She wrote this prayer in response to the question "How can I thank God for the trials in my life?"

> Father, you knew me before I was even in my mother's womb. You created my timeline, each hardship I encountered was a lesson learned. I strayed from you yet you never left me alone. You carried me into where I am today. You opened my eyes so I could see you, hear you, and feel you. Now I cling to you because I need you so much. You are my everything now. You have completed me and I thank you so much. Keep hold of my hand, dear Lord, don't let go. Without you I would be afraid. Stay with me. I want to walk with you.

Much of this prayer came from Psalm 139. This new believer was already praying the Word of God! I asked her to read it aloud to our small group. Tears fell down every cheek with each word she read. By exposing her heart to the Word of God, she began to make faith-filled choices in the midst of her messy life! We each had witnessed her metamorphosis. God had given us the privilege of participating in her amazing transformation. The most hopeful part of her story is reflected in this sentence: *I strayed from you, but you never left my side.*

God prompted me to share this experience for a reason. I know there is a Suzanne reading this story now. If you are like Suzanne, hungry and seeking something that you have seen in others, be courageous. Ask questions. Knock on doors. God will be faithful! Just a few months ago, I saw Suzanne sitting with a group of women around a table in a coffee shop, leading a Bible study . . . not attending but *leading*. God is faithful!

And if you are me, the one not listening to God's prompting, listen! Obey! Listen and obey so that you do not miss such a huge opportunity to be a part of leading someone closer to the heart of God.

I never write a study that God has not first walked me through myself. I wrote today's lesson because I, too, have experienced a transformation. And through that metamorphosis, God has given me the secrets of His kingdom, not to keep to myself and my small circle of friends, but to share. He called me years ago and continues to call me to study and teach His Word. Is He calling you too?

Listen and obey so that you do not miss such a huge opportunity to be a part of leading someone closer to the heart of God.

Is there someone to whom God is asking you to reach out and shine His light? If you are hesitating, ask God to help you step out in faith and begin a conversation. This will look different for everyone, depending on your situation. Pray for opportunity and for the words to begin the conversation. Pray for that person's heart to be prepared to receive what you have to say. I have prayed for God to be faithful as you step out to shine your light.

CONCLUDING THOUGHTS:

Jesus' three-year ministry with His disciples transformed their hearts and minds forever. His last words to them, and really to all believers, included this command: "Go and make disciples of all nations, baptizing them in the name of the Father and of the Son and of the Holy Spirit, and teaching them to obey everything I have commanded you" (Matthew 28:19–20 NIV). This is a clear call to shine our light into all the world.

Based on how God has spoken to your heart, complete the thought below.

Let your light shine so that . . .

PART TWO:
Giving

MEMORY VERSE: YOU ARE THE LIGHT OF THE WORLD . . . LET YOUR LIGHT SHINE BEFORE MEN, [SO] THAT THEY MAY SEE YOUR GOOD DEEDS AND PRAISE YOUR FATHER IN HEAVEN.

—Matthew 5:14, 16 (NIV; emphasis added)

This is your fifth and final memory verse! How does it feel to have four scriptures hidden in your heart? Congratulations! By the end of this week, you will have hidden five powerful "so that" scriptures in your heart. I am so proud of you! And I know God will bring them to mind when you need them for your own encouragement or someone else's.

When my husband and I got married, we had very different ideas about giving to the church. His family tithed weekly (gave 10 percent of their income to the church). And that is what my husband wanted to do. My family placed money in the offering plate each week, but the amount varied depending on what my dad had in his wallet. Both families gave.

I proposed waiting until the end of the month to calculate our church donation. If we had money remaining after paying our bills, I definitely believed it should go to the church. But Monty believed otherwise. When we married, we determined he would have primary responsibility for our finances. Some of that was due to the fact that math was not one of my strengths. Thus, the reason I chose law school. The only math required was adding up my billable hours!

So we began giving at the beginning of the month. This caused many heated discussions in our household . . . especially during the months when our bank account neared negative.

This disconnect continued in our marriage for years until I began to spend time in the Bible. God changed my perspective on giving the more I read and studied His Word. God revealed Himself and His character through different Old Testament names. Particular to the subject of giving, I learned the name *Yahweh Yireh* (Jehovah-Jireh), God our Provider. In the Hebrew, it means "Jehovah will see [to it]."

The Hebrew word *raah* (RA-ah, from which *yireh* is derived) means "to see, to observe, to perceive." When *raah* is used as part of God's name, it is translated "provide." Since God is omniscient (all-knowing) and able to see the future as well as the past and the present, this name tells us that He is able to anticipate and provide for whatever it is we need. Interestingly, the English word "provision" is made up of two Latin words that mean "to see beforehand." What God tells us in His name Jehovah-Jireh is that when we pray to Him, we are praying to our God who sees our situation beforehand, knows exactly what we need, and will provide it.

God made His name Jehovah-Jireh a reality in our marriage on numerous occasions through the years by miraculously providing for our family's needs, both financially and spiritually.

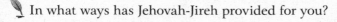 In what ways has Jehovah-Jireh provided for you?

⇒ APPLICATION:

Genesis 22 contains one of the most well-known Jehovah-Jireh stories in Scripture. But before we jump into this story, let's get some background information.

Read Genesis 12:1–5; 15:2–6; 17:1–8, 15–22.

God had promised Abraham a son at the age of one hundred. Listen to God's words to Abraham before his son was born:

> I will make you into a great nation and I will bless you; I will make your name great, and you will be a blessing. I will bless those who bless you, and whoever curses you I will curse; and all peoples on earth will be blessed through you. . . .
>
> Look up at the heavens and count the stars—if indeed you can count them . . . So shall your offspring be . . .
>
> Your wife Sarah will bear you a son, and you will call him Isaac. I will establish my covenant with him as an everlasting covenant for his descendants after him. (Genesis 12:2–3; 15:5; 17:19 NIV)

After Isaac was born, God came to Abraham again.

Read Genesis 22:1–19.

This time He commanded Abraham to take his son, the son God had promised him at one hundred years of age, and go up on a mountain and sacrifice him.

What do you think Abraham was thinking as he traveled up the mountain?

My first question would have been, *How can You ask me to take my own son's life?* But a more pressing and confusing question would have been, *Why would You ask me to sacrifice the very child through whom You promised to give me many descendants?*

If Abraham killed Isaac, how would God's promise be fulfilled?

Make no mistake about it: this was a test. Scripture plainly says in Genesis 22:1, "After a period of time, God decided to put Abraham to the test." It was a very real test designed to prove

Abraham's faith. God asked of him what seemed illogical and impossible . . . to give his son, Isaac, back to God.

Yes, Abraham had another son, Ishmael. But God had asked him to send Ishmael away because Isaac was the son of the promise. Now God was asking him to sacrifice his only remaining son. This was a true test of whether Abraham trusted God's promise and whether that trust was enough to cause him to obey.

What would you have done? Explain.

Thinking about my own sweet, blond-haired, blue-eyed, tenderhearted boy, I don't think I would have passed that test. I am certain I would have clung to my son for dear life and run the other way.

Don't think God didn't know what He was asking. God knew exactly what He was asking. He knew how special Isaac was to Abraham. Listen to God's words:

> Take your son, your only son Isaac **whom *I know* you love *deeply*,** and go to the land of Moriah. *When you get there,* I want you to offer Isaac to Me as a burnt offering on one of the mountains. I will show you which one. (Genesis 22:2; bold emphasis added)

"Abraham, light your son on fire and watch him burn." That is what God was asking of Abraham. This realization makes Abraham's response staggering—unimaginable, even—to most parents: he exhibited immediate and unquestioning obedience.

Reread Abraham's response in verses 3–9.

How could Abraham choose obedience so quickly? It is called faith, my friend. Our level of faith determines our response to God when He asks something of us. How we respond is overwhelming evidence of how strong our faith really is. Abraham's story is a powerful testimony of his faith. It reveals the kind of faith that pleases God . . . the kind of faith He blesses mightily.

Read Hebrews 11:17–19. How did Abraham reconcile God's command to sacrifice Isaac in his heart?

Abraham resolved in his heart long before that test to trust God. So when God spoke that day, Abraham did what he had learned to do: trust God to honor His Word. God made a covenant with Abraham. Isaac was the fulfillment of that covenant. Abraham reasoned that if God took Isaac, He would provide another way for His promise to be fulfilled. This trust is evidenced by Abraham's statement to his servants, "The boy and I will go over there. We will worship, and then **we** will come back to meet you *here*" (v. 5; bold emphasis added).

Imagine being present for this conversation between father and son in Genesis 22 when Isaac saw they had no lamb:

Isaac asked, "Father . . . where is the lamb for the burnt offering?" (v. 7).

Abraham responded, "God will provide the lamb . . . , my son" (v. 8).

He believed God would provide.

They continued their walk together.

Still no provision.

The next few passages are unbearable to read.

Abraham built an altar and "bound up his son Isaac" (v. 9).

Still no provision.

He "laid him on the altar on top of the stack of wood" (v. 9).

Still no provision.

Then he reached out his hand and took the knife to "kill his son" (v. 10).

Still no provision.

🖋 What are you feeling right now?

Finally, an angel of the Lord called out to Abraham from heaven, "Abraham! Abraham! . . . Don't lay your hand on the boy or do anything to *harm* him" (vv. 11–12).

Still no provision, but a word from the Lord.

🖋 What were the next words from the angel of the Lord? (v. 12)

Yes, this was a test. The angel of the Lord said, "I know now that you respect *the one True* God *and will be loyal to Him and follow His commands,* because you were willing to give up your son, your only son, to Me" (v. 12).

Abraham then looked up and saw a ram in the thicket.

Finally, God's provision.

The reason we are studying this story comes in the next passage:

He went over, dislodged the ram, and offered it up as a burnt offering in the place of his son. *From that day forward,* Abraham called that place, "The Eternal One will provide." Because of this, people still today say, "On the Mount of the Eternal, all will be provided." (vv. 13–14)

God began a covenant relationship that day with Abraham, a relationship that extends to us today.

The life of faith to which God calls us is not an easy one, friend. Like Noah, Abraham, David, Stephen, and Paul, we may be called to make some heartrending decisions, to walk a path we would rather not walk. The question for us at that point is . . . on what or on whom will we fix our confidence? These men all fixed it securely on God. Stories like Abraham's teach us that faith does not require an explanation. Faith rests on God's promises.

What is one of the most difficult sacrifices the Lord has asked of you? How did you respond? How did He provide?

God ended His visit with Abraham on Mount Moriah, confirming His covenant with Abraham:

Listen to the solemn vow the Eternal One has spoken: "Because you have done what I asked and were willing to give up your son, your only son, I will reaffirm My *covenant of* blessing to you *and your family.* I will make sure your descendants are as many as the stars of the heavens and the *grains of* sand on the shores. (Genesis 22:16–17)

God showered blessings upon Abraham for his obedience. He gave him great favor (v. 12), and He gave him back his son (v. 13). Abraham also learned a new name for God (v. 14), and he received new assurances from God (vv. 16–18). That, sweet friend, is how our God works.

He promises that blessings follow obedience.

✎ Fill in the blanks from the statement above and memorize it:
_____ follow _____ .

When God calls us to give of our time, our gifts, and/or our finances, so often we hesitate. *I'm too busy. It's just not the right time for me. We have too many financial commitments. We can't afford to give right now. Maybe next time. Maybe next year.*

✎ **Read each of these verses** and share the truths and/or promises you find.

> God is ready to overwhelm you with more blessings than you could ever imagine **so that** you'll always be taken care of in every way and you'll have more than enough to share. (2 Corinthians 9:8; bold emphasis added)

> You will be made rich in everything **so that** your generosity *will spill over in every direction. Through us* your generosity is at work inspiring praise and thanksgiving to God. (2 Corinthians 9:11; bold emphasis added)

> Command them to do good, to be rich in good deeds, and to be generous and willing to share. In this way they will lay up treasure for themselves as a firm foundation for the coming age, *so*

that they may take hold of the life that is truly life. (1 Timothy 6:18–19 NIV; emphasis added)

One of the greatest hindrances to being free to give generously to the work of God is the fear that we won't be able to meet our other needs. This is especially the case with financial giving. It was my fear early in my marriage.

Second Corinthians 8:9 in the NIV begins with three very important words.

Write the three words below.

Friend, this should be our starting point every time God asks us to take a step of faith.

Listen to the following scriptures that show the greatness of the God in whom we trust (bold emphasis has been added to each):

Job 42:2 says, "I know You can do **everything**; nothing You do can be foiled *or frustrated*."

Jeremiah 32:17 says, "Eternal Lord, with Your outstretched arm and Your enormous power You created the heavens and the earth. **Nothing** is too difficult for You."

One of the greatest hindrances to being free to give generously to the work of God is the fear that we won't be able to meet our other needs.

217

Matthew 19:26 says, "People cannot save themselves. But with God, **all** things are possible."

Luke 1:37 says, "So the impossible is **possible** with God."

Second Timothy 1:12 says, "I **know** Him and I have put my trust in Him. And I am **fully certain** that He has the ability to protect what I have placed in His care until that day."

There is nothing God will ask of us that He will not, in turn, provide. He provides because He not only wants to build our faith but also wants to ensure that we have everything we need to accomplish that which He calls us to do.

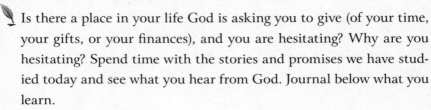 Is there a place in your life God is asking you to give (of your time, your gifts, or your finances), and you are hesitating? Why are you hesitating? Spend time with the stories and promises we have studied today and see what you hear from God. Journal below what you learn.

IF YOU WANT TO GO DEEPER:

Read 1 Timothy 6:17–19 from the New International Version. List at least five commands Paul instructs Timothy to tell those who are rich. What is the "so that" in verse 19?

Read Luke 12:13–21 in the NIV. How does the Parable of the Rich Fool speak to what Timothy is teaching the rich?

I take great delight in what Paul instructs Timothy to say to the wealthy at the end 1 Timothy 6:17. He says God provides us with everything for our enjoyment. God wants us to enjoy life and enjoy His blessings! But we must do so with the idea of bringing Him glory as part of that enjoyment.

We must hold our wealth with open hands and open hearts and prayerfully ask God how to spend what He has so generously given. God expects us to look for ways to use our wealth to do good things for the least in the kingdom. He invites us to share our wealth with others, including friends and family. In this way people will see, and even experience, the generosity and provision of Jehovah-Jireh through us.

We should also be smart and put God's money to work. When we follow these instructions, we enrich ourselves spiritually, and we make investments for future use.

What do the following verses teach us about the attitude God wants us to have toward material things?

1. Proverbs 8:17–21

2. Proverbs 30:7–9

3. Ecclesiastes 5:10–11

4. Matthew 6:19–21, 24

⇒⇒ CONCLUDING THOUGHTS:

Today we focused on giving.

Based on how God has spoken to your heart today, complete the thought below.

Let your light shine so that . . .

PART THREE:
Loving the Unlovable

MEMORY VERSE: YOU ARE THE LIGHT OF THE WORLD . . . LET YOUR LIGHT SHINE BEFORE MEN, **[SO] THAT** THEY MAY SEE YOUR GOOD DEEDS AND PRAISE YOUR FATHER IN HEAVEN.

—Matthew 5:14, 16 (NIV; emphasis added)

WALK IN THE POWER OF THE TRUTH THAT THE NAME OF THE LORD GOD MAY BE GLORIFIED AMONG YOU, HIS RENOWN MAY BE SEEN IN YOU AND AMONG YOU, AND ALL THE WORLD MAY BE ASTONISHED.

—George Fox, leader of the Quakers[1]

Whatever our calling, wherever God has placed us, He calls each of us to live a life set apart . . . to let our light shine *so that* God may be seen and glorified. Can you think of a more powerful and effective way to bring God glory than to love the unlovable?

Paul continually prayed for God's people to know His love and to live a life of love:

> May love be *the rich soil* where their lives take root. May it be the bedrock where their lives are founded *so that together* with all of Your people they will have the power to understand that the love of the Anointed is infinitely long, wide, high, and deep, surpassing everything anyone previously experienced. God, may Your fullness flood through their entire beings. (Ephesians 3:17–19)

> Here's what I pray for you: *Father,* may their love grow more and more in wisdom and insight. (Philippians 1:9)

May the Lord flood you with an *unending, undying* love for one another and for all humanity, like our love for you. (1 Thessalonians 3:12)

Why are we called to live a life of love?

Read John 13:34–35. What does Jesus say on the subject of loving others?

John Piper wrote on this subject, "One indispensable public mark of a Christian is love for other Christians. Jesus assumes the world is watching this and that judgments are being made. He means it to be this way."[2]

We are God's people, His ambassadors. When we demonstrate love in this world, we give the world a compelling picture of God . . . one that draws them toward Him and not away.

But we can't demonstrate what we don't know. To genuinely love others, we must know, believe, and accept deep in the recesses of our own hearts the unconditional, lavish love of God.

Jesus' death on the cross at Calvary is the ultimate expression of God's love:

But *think about this:* while we were wasting our lives in sin, God revealed His powerful love to us *in a tangible display*—the Anointed One died for us. (Romans 5:8)

Sin prevents us from being in relationship with a righteous, holy God. To rectify this seemingly impossible situation, God punished His Son for our sin. He willingly put Jesus to death to restore the intimate relationship He once had with His creation in the garden of Eden. This sacrificial gift reveals how much God loves us!

First John 4:19 teaches, "We love because He has first loved us." All love ultimately comes from God.

We cannot know love if we don't know God. We cannot give His love away if we have not experienced His love. Once we know and experience God's love, His love is made complete in us (1 John 4:12).

In Matthew 22:37–40, Jesus spoke very clearly on love. Quoting from Scripture, He said, "'Love the Eternal One your God with all your heart and all your soul and all your mind.' This is the first and greatest commandment." Then He continued with the second greatest commandment: "'Love your neighbor as yourself.' The rest of the law, and all the teachings of the prophets, are but variations on these themes."

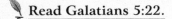 **Read Mark 12:29–31.** When asked by a teacher of the law which commandment was most important, what did Jesus answer?

When we arrive at this place of receiving God's love and loving Him back, then and only then is God able to love others through us.

APPLICATION:

How does God's love get inside of us?

Read Galatians 5:22.

Write the fruit of the Spirit below.

Love is a fruit of the Holy Spirit. When we declare our love for God, confess our sin, repent of it, and turn our lives over to Christ, He seals us with His Holy Spirit (2 Corinthians 1:22). God indwells our hearts and begins to produce His fruit in us. God, through the power of His Holy Spirit, deposits His love in our hearts (Galatians 5:22).

When His love comes alive in us, it takes root. It begins to blossom and grow. The deeper the roots go down, the deeper our ability to express that love.

Friend, if we want more of God's love, we must pray for it. But we must also dig deep into His Word, inviting Him to teach us how to love others. As we hide His Word in our hearts and pray for opportunities to love others, God will create opportunities for this to happen.

Read the following passages and share what they teach about loving others.

1. Ephesians 4:29, 31–32

2. Ephesians 5:1

3. 1 Peter 4:8

4. 1 John 4:20–21

In the midst of messy lives and messy relationships, loving people this way is just plain hard, especially when it comes to difficult people. But are they really difficult people? In her book, *The Beloved Disciple: Following John to the Heart of Jesus,* Beth Moore suggests that maybe such people are not really "difficult people." "When I began this chapter," she wrote in the middle of chapter 33, "I intended to use the phrase 'loving difficult people,' but under the direction of the Holy Spirit, I changed the description to 'loving people we find difficult.' . . . Just because we find someone difficult to love doesn't make him, or her, a difficult person."[3] The problem could be with us and not them.

Humility is an essential ingredient for loving others. We will spend more time on humility later. But for now, we will examine humility as it relates to love.

If we find ourselves angry with or hurt by another, before we let loose with our tongues, we must examine our own hearts. It may be God is working on our heart, not theirs. God will always deal with us first. Remember, we are created in His image. God seeks through every life experience to refine us more and more so that one day we perfectly reflect His image. That process necessitates getting rid of anything and everything in us that does not reflect His image. As we submit to His refining and allow God to transform our hearts and minds, we will find it easier to love the unlovable.

What about the times when the one with whom we are struggling really is difficult? It is then that we must pull from the truths we studied above. We must love with a love outside ourselves. We must draw from God's love.

God's love is *agapaō agape*. This kind of love requires a deliberate choice to love no matter how we feel. There is another love, *phileō philos* love, that is based more on feelings. *Philos* love develops as we get to know someone, like a best friend or a boyfriend.

To love the unlovable means we must make a deliberate choice to love someone despite how we feel about her. This cannot be done in our own strength. It can only be done by drawing from the *agape* love within us. It necessitates choosing our will over our emotions.

It helps me understand this love more when I remember that sometimes (maybe lots of times, depending on who you ask) I, too, am unlovely and unlovable. Yet God still loves me with a powerful and everlasting love.

> We must love with a love outside ourselves. We must draw from God's love.

Loving someone who is unlovable challenges us to live beyond what we can do in and through our own strength. It requires that we press into God. It demands a conscious decision to rid our hearts and minds of all toxic thoughts regarding the person and replace them with the truths of Scripture. When we empty ourselves of these thoughts, we make room for more positive thoughts. With more of God's Word and Spirit indwelling us, we will more often make the faith-filled choice to choose words and actions that reflect love, not hate.

But we must be aware of our enemy, the evil one. He will come after us with lies. He will remind us how this person or that person has hurt us. He will replay his hurtful words. He will tell us she doesn't deserve our love and understanding. He will tell us not to risk our hearts again. He will tell us not to let that individual hurt us again.

Friend, when you hear these lies, take them captive (2 Corinthians 10:5). Don't let them even enter into your mind. Listen only to the One who is Truth, Jesus. Satan does not know love. He can never know love. He can never know truth. Remember, he is a liar and the father of lies. In him there is no truth at all (John 8:44).

Listen to the truth of God's Word. Choose love.

God will be faithful with the love you pour out on one who is undeserving and unlovely. Remember, blessings follow obedience. He will bless you tenfold for your obedience. He will reward you, friend. It is when we extend God's *agape* love that we shine His light into this broken and hurting world and bring Him some of the greatest glory and honor and praise.

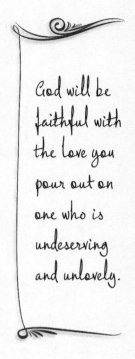

God will be faithful with the love you pour out on one who is undeserving and unlovely.

IF YOU WANT TO GO DEEPER:

Read Romans 12:9–18.

Loving others, especially the most unlovable and those from whom we get nothing in return, is the true mark of a believer. The New Testament contains more than fifty commands to love. Loving others is not an option, my friend. It is a command.

In this passage from Romans, Paul calls us to love one another, to love our neighbors, and even to love our enemies.

Read through each of the following verses in this passage and share Paul's message to us about love. Share one way you can live out these instructions in your own life.

living so that

1. Verse 9

2. Verse 10

3. Verse 13

4. Verse 14

5. Verse 15

6. Verse 16

Go back through the verses and choose one with which you struggle the most. Spend some time with the Lord, asking Him to help you obey this instruction. Take steps over the next few weeks to put into practice this instruction, and journal how God works in your life as you walk in obedience.

CONCLUDING THOUGHTS:

In this lesson, we focused on loving the unlovable.

Based on how God has spoken to your heart, complete the thought below.

Let your light shine so that . . .

PART FOUR:
Choosing Forgiveness

MEMORY VERSE: YOU ARE THE LIGHT OF THE WORLD . . . LET YOUR LIGHT SHINE BEFORE MEN, **[SO] THAT** THEY MAY SEE YOUR GOOD DEEDS AND PRAISE YOUR FATHER IN HEAVEN.

–Matthew 5:14, 16 (NIV; emphasis added)

Some of the messiest parts of our lives stem from refusing to extend forgiveness to another.

Anger welled up within me. How dare she ask this of me . . . of us? I reread her e-mail, which only fueled my fury. Rather than reply immediately, I decided to forward her e-mail to my husband for his advice. In my current state, any words I would have written to her directly would have been unkind.

I poured out my "how dare she" thoughts. Bitterness took root as I typed and typed, spewing all my pent-up frustration. When I finished, I reread my message with great satisfaction. I'd expressed myself well in a safe place to a safe person. Then I pressed send.

In that moment, I glanced at the "to" box. I could not believe my eyes! Instead of hitting "forward," I'd hit "reply." My heart sank. All my hurtful words, all my vented anger, en route to this woman, not my husband.

I felt sick. Never had I experienced the myriad of emotions that filled my heart.

What should I do? I called my husband and asked for his wisdom. We both agreed that I needed to e-mail her, explain what happened, and ask forgiveness. It was the hardest e-mail I've ever written.

> Some of the messiest parts of our lives stem from refusing to extend forgiveness to another.

Have you ever experienced a time like this in your life? Explain.

How did you respond?

APPLICATION:

Forgiveness is a choice. Before we begin today, honestly answer these questions:

- Do you harbor unforgiveness in your heart?
- Is there someone from whom you need to ask forgiveness?

As we proceed through this lesson, prayerfully ask the Lord to be at work in your heart with regard to these questions. Ask Him what He is trying to teach you and what steps He may want you to take. Today is a divine appointment for you, my friend. Be encouraged because God has a "word" just for you.

For some of you, He wants to set you free!

Nancy Leigh DeMoss, in her book *Choosing Forgiveness: Your Journey to Freedom,* has written, "Forgiveness is not a method to be learned as much as a truth to be lived."[4] What a powerful statement!

We live in a fallen world and continually interact with people who hurt, offend, and even lie to us. Knowing this, the crucial issue becomes, how will we respond? God cares about our response. He calls us to one response and one response only: forgiveness. When we respond in obedience, when we choose forgiveness, God sets us free from the bitterness that holds us captive. Choosing forgiveness allows God to mold our hearts into beautiful vessels of grace and forgiveness.

🖊 **Read Colossians 3:13.** Write it below.

🖊 Why are we to forgive?

God does not give any other option, my friend.

🖊 **Read Mark 11:25.**

🖊 What is the "so that"?

Notice the words used by Mark. "If you hold *anything* against *anyone*" (NIV; emphasis added).

God's Word is clear. God calls us to forgive, no matter the offense, even the most horrific of crimes or circumstances. Why? Because harboring unforgiveness interrupts our fellowship with God. Refusing to forgive prevents us from experiencing the fullness of God's presence in our lives. He cannot work in a heart shackled by unforgiveness. His fruit cannot flourish in a heart bound in unforgiveness. Bitterness keeps us from receiving the fullness of God's fruit—love, joy, peace, patience, kindheartedness, goodness, gentleness, faithfulness, and self-control (Galatians 6:22–23). Unforgiveness and the fruit of the Spirit cannot coexist in one heart. One will always reign victorious over the other.

Is God pricking your heart? Is a name coming to mind?

Be encouraged. You are not alone. Forgiveness is hard, and it doesn't come naturally. When my son was younger, he often played pickup basketball after school. On a daily basis, the moms witnessed arguments over who fouled whom and whose rules were wrong and whose were right. Generally, I tried to stay out of these skirmishes. One afternoon, however, tempers flew to the point that I felt I had to intervene. I called my son out of the game and encouraged him to offer the first apology. His big blue eyes looked up at me, pleading not to have to be the one to say, "I'm sorry." I told him that I would not make him, but that I trusted he would "make the right choice" . . . the words all children dread hearing. I watched as he grudgingly walked over to his friend, now turned enemy, and grumbled, "I'm sorry." No eye contact, no handshake, no smile, not a semblance of remorse or repentance.

That, my friend, is what comes naturally. A begrudging heart. But God wants so much more. He desires genuine, heartfelt forgiveness. This kind of forgiveness comes from deep within our souls. It's not a shallow apology composed of a few curt words. Rather, it's the kind of apology that physically hurts as we speak the words.

This kind of apology is the only way to rid our hearts and minds of the poison left behind by

> Unforgiveness and the fruit of the Spirit cannot coexist in one heart. One will always reign victorious over the other.

bitterness and unforgiveness. Words of forgiveness are the only way to true healing and wholeness.

How can we truly come to this place of forgiveness?

First, what helped me forgive my rapist is remembering that in forgiving, God was not asking me to forget. The injustice, the pain, the betrayal, our hurt, and our pain are valid in His eyes. They are real. God understands them. He stands ready to minister healing to our wounds. But what He is asking us to do is to allow *Him* to exact justice. He is the Judge. Psalm 7:11 says, "God is a just judge." Judging right and wrong is His role, not ours. Beth Moore wrote in *Breaking Free: Making Liberty in Christ a Reality in Life* that forgiving means "handing over to God the responsibility for justice."[5]

Romans 12:17–19 says:

> Do not retaliate with evil, regardless of the evil brought against you. Try to do what is good *and right and honorable* as agreed upon by all people. **If it is within your power**, make peace with all people. *Again,* my loved ones, do not seek revenge; instead, allow God's wrath *to make sure justice is served. Turn it over to Him.* For the Scriptures say, "Revenge is Mine. I will settle all scores." (bold emphasis added)

We do not need to do God's work for Him. We must trust Him with His job. He is the just Judge (Psalm 7:11; 2 Timothy 4:8). You are not giving your offender a pass, sweet friend. You are handing him or her over to the only One who can exact true justice.

I speak from experience. Forgiving sets us free!

Forgiving our offender makes room for God's peace to blossom and grow, the peace that stands watch over our hearts and minds (Philippians 4:7).

Second, what enabled me to forgive is remembering how much God has forgiven me. Jesus brings this truth alive in His parable of the unforgiving servant found in Matthew 18:23–35.

🪶 **Read this parable.**

🪶 How did the king respond? How did the forgiven servant respond to his servant?

🪶 How did it make you feel as you read the forgiven servant's response?

As I struggled with forgiving my attacker, God placed this parable before me. Bitterness and hatred had consumed my heart for years. I justified my emotions because of all my attacker had stolen from me: my dignity, my security, my confidence, my trust, my joy, and my peace. But as I read this story, in the quietness of my heart I heard God say, *You are the unforgiving servant.* In light of how much God had forgiven me, how could I not forgive what had been done to me? This man had already stolen years from my life; would I continue to allow him to take more? I knew that I would never receive the full and complete healing God had in store for me until I fully forgave my attacker.

> I will never forget the day. I sat alone on my sofa in the living room, speaking to a man who was not there. I could not see, feel or touch him, yet I forgave him. I had no idea the depth of seething hatred and bitterness that entangled my heart until I spoke the words. Cleansing tears flowed down my cheeks like a never-ending fountain. As I cried, my chest heaved up and down, almost to the point of my being unable to breathe. I forgave my attacker not only for everything he did to me, but also for

everything he had stolen from me. In that moment, God lifted a huge weight from my shoulders. A precious peace fell upon me.[6]

Make no mistake about it. Our willingness to extend forgiveness is proportionally related to the depth of our understanding of what Jesus did for us on the cross. Many of us struggle with forgiveness because we do not grasp the enormity of the grace God extended us on Calvary. Without that knowledge and without the willingness to forgive that flows from it, we will never receive the fullness of God's peace and blessings.

Finally, forgiveness came more easily as I studied the tragic consequences of living with a heart burdened by unforgiveness.

Hear this warning loud and clear: unforgiveness gives the devil a foothold in our hearts and in our relationships.

Read 2 Corinthians 2:5–11. What has happened in this passage?

The Corinthian church had taken disciplinary action against one of its own members. Paul learned that some in the church wanted to inflict further punishment on the offender.

What is Paul's word to the church on forgiveness?

Because Paul had determined the man being punished was truly sorry and that to punish him further would do more harm than good, he urged the church not only to forgive but also to move beyond forgiveness and comfort this man.

🖋 What does Paul warn will happen if we do not forgive? (v. 11)

The devil loves strife and division. One of his names is "divider." When he sees a stronghold like unforgiveness take hold in a person's heart, he celebrates. It allows him to gain a foothold. He wins. And believe me: he holds on tight. He will fight to keep you bound up in unforgiveness. He will fill your mind with lies. He will desensitize your heart to God's voice. This is why Paul warns us in Ephesians 4:26–27: "When you are angry, don't let it carry you into sin. Don't let the sun set with anger in your heart or give the devil room to work."

Satan uses our anger to draw us farther from the heart of God, and to plant a root of bitterness in our hearts. Hebrews issues a similar warning: "Watch carefully that no one falls short of God's favor, that no well of bitterness springs up to trouble you and throw many others off the path" (Hebrews 12:15).

The NIV uses the term "root" of bitterness. Again, we have a choice:

- the faith-filled choice: when we feel offended, we can go to God, give Him the hurt, and ask for His help

or

- the faith-less choice: we can resist God, hold on to the hurt, and deal with it ourselves.

If we take the latter route, bitterness will fester and take root; it will spring up and cause greater trouble, not only for us but for those close to us.

Bitterness is like poison. It infects every part of our lives. Even though feelings of resentment, anger, and unforgiveness seem justified, they are not. They are destructive. And the only antidote for their poison is the Word of God. Draw near to God through His Word, and you will find the mercy, grace, and strength to help you forgive (Hebrews 4:16).

Let God's grace, not bitterness, flow through you. There truly is no greater witness of God's love in a person's life than when she extends forgiveness. This choice, and this choice alone, brings peace to our hearts and glory and honor and praise to our Father in heaven!

If you have identified a person against whom you harbor unforgiveness, I invite you to take a step toward extending forgiveness. What this looks like will be different for each one of you. Maybe your hurt is so deep or so fresh that you simply need to begin to pray for God to soften your heart toward your offender. Maybe you cannot physically be with him or her, so you may have to do as I did on my living room sofa that day. Perhaps you are ready to forgive. You may want to write a letter or make a phone call. If the person is close, schedule a visit. Prayerfully ask God what your next step is, and ask Him to equip you with everything you need to walk in obedience to His command to forgive. He will be faithful!

CONCLUDING THOUGHTS:

Let's return to my opening story about my e-mail. I sent my e-mail asking forgiveness. Her gracious and forgiving response astounded me. She thanked me for my apology and ended with these words: "I forgive you, so let's just put this behind us." Her words of forgiveness melted the bitterness that had consumed my heart just an hour before. I'm sure she was hurt. My words were harsh. Yet, she chose to overlook and forgive my offense. By choosing forgiveness, she extended grace and prevented a bitter root from taking hold.

From that day forward, I have prayed for God's grace, not bitterness, to flow through me.

My friend's gracious decision to forgive prevented Satan from gaining a foothold in our friendship. It also modeled humility. Her choice to forgive has forever changed how my heart will react toward others who offend me.

Unforgiveness erects walls. It severs relationships. It creates division and strife.

Forgiveness tears down walls. It mends relationships. It builds unity and peace.

My friend's response tore down the wall I had erected. It mended our relationship. It brought unity and peace. We continued to work together for years after that event. How difficult and awkward it would have been if she had not extended forgiveness and had, instead, held a grudge. She set an example for me that day. She taught me a huge lesson on forgiveness. She represented Christ well that day. She let her light shine brightly and brought glory and honor and praise to God.

Based on how God has spoken to your heart, complete the thought below.

Let your light shine so that . . .

PART FIVE:
Humility

MEMORY VERSE: YOU ARE THE LIGHT OF THE WORLD . . . LET YOUR LIGHT SHINE BEFORE MEN, **[SO] THAT** THEY MAY SEE YOUR GOOD DEEDS AND PRAISE YOUR FATHER IN HEAVEN.

–Matthew 5:14, 16 (NIV; emphasis added)

We have reached the end of our study. How can it be? Mixed emotions fill my heart as I write these final words. I am thrilled to be finished, yet sad too . . . like when I have read a good book and don't want it to end. When I sat down to write, I wondered how it would ever come together . . . so many topics, so many scriptures, so many truths. But God was faithful. He took every prayer I whispered, every hour I researched, every verse I studied, and faithfully supplied the words needed to create *Living So That*. Thank you for taking this journey through God's Word with me. I will miss you and look forward to our next study together.

We end our time together studying Jesus' words on humility.

Define humility.

Who in your sphere of influence comes to mind when you think of "humility"? What is it about them that exemplifies humility?

Jeremy Taylor, a seventeenth-century ordained priest and prolific writer, gave this enlightening insight on humility: "Humility
begins as a *gift* from God, but it is increased as a *habit* we develop."[7]

 Explain what the author meant by these words.

APPLICATION:

Paul taught us in an earlier lesson that God's power operates most
powerfully and effectively in our weakness.

 What do these characters' stories teach you about the kind of person God calls to do His kingdom work?

1. Moses (Exodus 3:1–15; 4:1–17)

2. Gideon (Judges 6)

3. David (1 Samuel 16:1–13)

God rarely uses the wise, the mighty, the noble, the wealthy, or the powerful to do His kingdom work. And when He does choose someone like this, that person usually endures an unpleasant season of humbling at His hands.

Read 1 Corinthians 1:26–29.

> Look carefully at your call, brothers and sisters. By human standards, not many of you are deemed to be wise. Not many are considered powerful. Not many of you come from royalty, right? But *celebrate this:* God selected the world's foolish to bring shame upon *those who think they are* wise; likewise, He selected the world's weak to bring disgrace upon *those who think they are* strong. God selected the common and the castoff, whatever lacks status, **so [that]** He could invalidate the claims of those who think those things are significant. So it makes no sense for any person to boast in God's presence. (bold emphasis added)

To whom is Paul speaking?

Whom does Paul say the Lord chooses? (vv. 27–28)

God does this *so that* . . . ? (v. 29)

In God's economy, humility is not only commanded but also valued and rewarded. First Peter 5:5–6 says:

> All of you, clothe yourselves with humility toward one another, because, "God opposes the proud but gives grace to the humble." Humble yourselves, therefore, under God's mighty right hand, *[so] that* he may lift you up in due time. (NIV; emphasis added)

"Clothe" is a translation of the Greek word *egkomboomai* and means "to gird oneself with a thing, to be clothed with." "Gird" means "to encircle or bind with a belt or band; to surround; enclose; hem in." We see this same word in John 13, when Jesus washed His disciples' feet. The King James Version says, "He riseth from supper, and laid aside his garments; and took a towel, and girded himself. After that he poureth water into a bason, and began to wash the disciples' feet, and to wipe them with the towel wherewith he was girded" (John 13:4–5).

In Jesus' time, it was a mark of honor for a host to provide a servant to wash a guest's feet. Such a servant often wore a slave's apron or towel around his waist. Before Jesus began to wash His disciples' feet, He removed His outer garment and wrapped a similar towel around His waist. In doing this, Jesus modeled servanthood for His disciples.

Peter used the word "girded" here to teach us that just as Jesus laid aside His outer garments and put on a towel to become a servant, so each of us should "put on" a servant's attitude and minister to one another. Jesus' example teaches that humility is not demeaning ourselves; rather, it's *honoring* others and not thinking of ourselves at all!

"Humility" is a translation of the Greek word *tapeinophrosune*, defined as "a virtue, a fruit of the gospel, that exists when a person

In God's economy, humility is not only commanded but also valued and rewarded.

through most genuine self-evaluation deems himself worthless." Humility does not focus on our sinfulness as much as it does how we view ourselves in relation to God. God wants us absolutely dependent upon Him, unfettered to the things of this world.

🖊 **Read Philippians 2:1–11** for a biblical definition of humility. What is Christ's attitude?

> Don't let selfishness and prideful agendas take over. Embrace true humility, and lift your heads to extend love to others. Get beyond yourselves and protecting your own interests; *be sincere,* and secure your neighbors' interests first.
>
> *In other words,* adopt the mind-set of Jesus the Anointed. *Live with His attitude in your hearts. Remember:*
>
> > Though He was in the form of God,
> >   He chose not to cling to equality with God;
> > But He poured Himself out *to fill a vessel brand new*;
> >   a servant in form
> >   and a man indeed.
> > The very likeness of humanity. (Philippians 2:3–7)

🖊 What did God do in response to Jesus' humble, obedient acts? (vv. 9–11)

My son is fifteen, six foot three, and a good basketball player, but he still has much to learn. Sometimes he forgets. We tell him that his ability to play is a gift from God, something to be developed and appreciated, something that can be taken away at any time. When he has performed well on the court, whether in a school game, a rec game, or with friends, he loves to talk about it. My husband speaks the same mantra after every game: "Bo, it's great to celebrate how you have played with us, because we are your family. But with everyone else, never, ever celebrate your own performance. Let others compliment you." Proverbs 27:2 says, "Let someone else praise you; *compliments are always sweeter from* a stranger's lips than from your own."

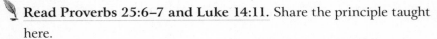 **Read Proverbs 25:6–7 and Luke 14:11.** Share the principle taught here.

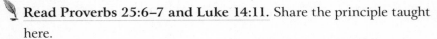 Write Luke 14:11 below. Give one example of how you can live this out in your life this week.

Humility will never be a reality until we fully submit every area of our hearts to God, holding back nothing. Those who are prideful cannot receive God's grace. Their hardened hearts are callous and unreceptive to God's love.

Proverbs 3:34 says, "God *treats the arrogant as they treat others,* mocking the mockers, *scorning the scornful,* but He pours out His grace on the humble." James 4:6 echoes, "God opposes the proud, but He pours out grace on the humble."

living so that ❦

🪶 **Read Proverbs 6:16–17 and 8:13.** What does God hate?

Pride turned Lucifer, the angel of light, into Satan. Pride caused Eve to eat the forbidden fruit. Pride caused the downfall of human-kind and continues to contribute to its downfall today. The only remedy is grace. Once we experience God's grace, it should lead us to yield ourselves first to God and then to one another.

🪶 List evidence of humility.

We started this lesson with Jeremy Taylor's words that humility is a gift and a habit that must be developed. What are some ways we develop this habit?

- First, pray for a humble heart.

  Ask God to give you a submissive and obedient heart.

- Second, revere God above all else.

  Have a right view of who you are in relation to God.

- Third, submit to God's will.

  Put aside your agenda and desire His will above all else.

● Fourth, walk in obedience to God's Word.

It is eternal, immutable truth, written to guide us into all wisdom, knowledge, and revelation.

● Fifth, confess your sin daily.

The Bible promises that when we confess our sins, God is "faithful and just to forgive" (1 John 1:9 KJV). This means admitting our faults and not making excuses; it also means bearing criticism and looking for the truth in it, if any.

● Sixth, think of others as better than yourself.

Put others' needs before your own.

● Seventh, do good expecting nothing in return.

Seek only your Father's praise. When you receive praise, give it back to the Lord.

Satan uses pride more than any other emotion, so be alert and aware of his schemes. Don't fall for his lies and deception. He wants nothing more than to draw you to a place of pride. He will come after you as he did Eve, King Saul, and even Jesus. He tempted Jesus in the wilderness, so how much more will he come after us?

🖋 Prayerfully look over this list. Is there an area or areas in which you need to work? Ask God to help you develop this godly virtue of humility and to work on this area with His help.

Friend, God promises a great "so that" when we do humble ourselves:

> Humble yourselves therefore under the mighty hand of God, *[so] that* he may exalt you in due time. (1 Peter 5:6 KJV; emphasis added)

To "exalt" means "to elevate, lift up"—and those who humble themselves before the Lord will be *exalted*!

The key phrase in this promise is found in the words "in due time." God will not exalt us until we are ready. Sometimes a time of waiting precedes the "lifting up." We have to walk through the messiness of life before we are ready for God to lavish His great favor upon us.

We find examples throughout Scripture. Jesus endured years of rejection, persecution, and even death on a cross before He sat down at the right hand of God. Moses endured times of isolation, persecution, and difficult trials before God used him to deliver the Jews. Joseph suffered persecution, wrongful imprisonment, and separation from family and friends before God elevated him to the throne. David waited decades, enduring numerous trials and tribulations, including attempts on his life, before God crowned him king of Judah.

Humility requires patience. But in the end, God rewards our patience.

"I have set you an example *[so] that* you should do as I have done for you. I tell you the truth, no servant is greater than his master, nor is a messenger greater than the one who sent him. Now that you know these things, *you will be blessed if you do them.*" (John 13:15–17 NIV; emphasis added)

🖋 **Reread Luke 14:7–11.**

🖋 In what ways does this parable affirm the lesson we learned on humility?

🖋 How will you apply what you learned in this parable practically?

🖋 I encourage you to make it a priority to give someone else honor. Journal what happened and how it made you feel. How did God use it?

⇉ IF YOU WANT TO GO DEEPER:

After the wonderful truths and promises we have studied, allow me to share one last powerful truth.

Our final "so that" comes from Luke 12.

Be dressed ready for service and keep your lamps burning, like men waiting for their master to return from a wedding banquet, *so that* when he comes and knocks they can immediately open the door for him. (vv. 35–36 NIV; emphasis added)

The powerful truth is this: Christ is coming back! He came first as a Savior. And He promises He will come again.

When the Son of Man comes, *He will be as visible* as lightning in the East is visible even in the West . . . That is when the sign of the Son of Man will appear in the sky. All the nations of the earth will mourn. They will see the Son of Man coming; they will see Him powerful and glorious, *riding on chariots* of clouds in the sky. With a loud trumpet call, He will send out *battalions of* heavenly messengers; and they will gather His *beloved faithful* elect from the four corners of creation, from one end of heaven to the other. (Matthew 24:27, 30–31)

But the next time He will return as a Judge, a Warrior, and a King.

I looked up and saw that heaven had opened. Suddenly, a white horse appeared. Its rider is called Faithful and True, and with righteousness He exercises judgment and wages war. His eyes burn like a flaming fire, and on His head are many crowns. His name was written *before the creation of the world,* and no one knew it except He Himself. He is dressed in a robe dipped in blood, *and* the name He was known by is The Word of God. And the armies of heaven, outfitted in fine linen, white and pure, were following behind Him on white steeds. From His mouth darts a sharp sword with which to strike down the nations. He will rule over them with a scepter made of iron. He will trample the winepress of the fury of the wrath of God, the All Powerful. And there on His robe and on His thigh was written His name: King of kings and Lord of lords. (Revelation 19:11–16)

Second Thessalonians 1:6–7 says:

God is just: He will pay back trouble to those who trouble you and give relief to you who are troubled, and to us as well. This will happen when the Lord Jesus is revealed from heaven in blazing fire with his powerful angels. (NIV)

Christ is coming back, my friend. When He does, it will not be quietly. Every eye will see. Every ear will hear. Every nation will fear. Every knee will bow. And every tongue will confess that He is Lord.

How will this happen? We cannot fathom. What will it sound like? We do not know. What will it feel like? We cannot imagine. When will it be? The date is unknown.

But we are told one thing. We must be ready. Let's revisit Luke 12 again.

Be dressed ready for service and keep your lamps burning, like men waiting for their master to return from a wedding banquet, *so that* when he comes and knocks they can immediately open the door for him. (vv. 35–36 NIV; emphasis added)

In Jesus' time, Jewish weddings were held at night. The bridegroom's servants stayed awake, waiting late into the night for their master to bring home his new bride. The servants never knew the exact time of their arrival, so they stood, with their robes girded up, ready to welcome and serve them.

We are to do the same. We are to keep our lamps burning. Remember our memory verse for this week? It says to let our light shine before men. We are to continually let our lights shine by

> Christ is coming back, my friend. When He does, it will not be quietly.

loving and serving others. We are not to "let up" because the master is away.

Living this way keeps us close to the heart of God. It ensures that we are continually looking and listening for His voice, for ways He can minister to and use us. God desires we have an acute awareness of His presence 24/7. When we live this way, we will not be caught off guard when He comes. We will be ready.

Read Luke 12:37. What will happen for those whom He finds with their lamps burning?

I could barely take in the words as I read the end of this verse. It says that when the Master returns, those He finds ready and waiting will recline at a table, and *He will wait on them* (NIV). Remember, in the Jewish tradition, the servants treated the bride and groom like royalty. The servants served them. It would never be expected that the groom would serve the staff. Yet Luke tells us that our King, the King of kings and Lord of lords, will minister to His faithful servants. He will reward the ready and faithful ones. The Master reverses the roles. He will serve the servants!

This verse gives us another message as well. It is yet another message to "be alert," "to watch." We are not to be caught by surprise by the Lord's second coming. He has told us He will come. He will be like a thief, unannounced and unexpected. But He will come (Matthew 24:43–44; 1 Thessalonians 5:2). Matthew 24:36 tells us that no one knows the day or hour, not even the Son, but only the Father.

We must be ready!

»»CONCLUDING THOUGHTS:

We have spent five weeks studying God's call to *Living So That.* I have shared much of the messiness in my own life and challenged you to examine and share yours. We have learned through the "so that" verses how to transform our hearts and minds, how to make more faith-filled choices and fewer faith-less choices in the midst of our messy lives. We have completed five "Calls to Action"—ways we can be working while we are "in the wait." Friend, we have learned that we must be about God's work so that we can be found faithful when He comes again.

Paul wrote in 1 Corinthians 4:1–2:

> *Rather than power brokers,* think of us as servants of the Anointed One, *the Liberating King,* caretakers of the mysteries of God. Because we are in this particular role, it is especially important that we are people of fidelity and integrity.

God desires readiness and faithfulness. Let's make it our heart's desire to live in this ready state so that we will be found faithful upon His return.

Our "so thats" will vary, but the way He works them into our lives is the same. He starts with commands from His Word that require small steps of obedience. When we are faithful with these small steps, He will ask more of us. Each step calls us out of our comfort zones to go deeper still with Him, whether it be trusting in Him for salvation, trusting Him to honor His Word, trusting Him in prayer, trusting Him in a trial, or trusting Him to enable us to live our faith out loud for all to see.

We have learned much. Please don't let your time in the Word end here. Stay in God's Word.

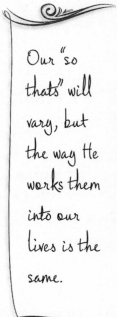

Our "so thats" will vary, but the way He works them into our lives is the same.

Continue your search for more "so thats." And most important, follow through with your "Calls to Action."

God specially designed each one of us to do kingdom work. We have God-given gifts and talents, assigned to us before time began, to enable us to do that work (Ephesians 2:10). Living according to the "so that" verses is God's way of guiding us toward those plans. He will use these verses to point us in the direction He is leading.

Heather, I saved you so that . . .

Mary, believe My Word so that . . .

Noelle, pray so that . . .

Veronica, trust Me in this trial so that . . .

Lisa, live out My Word on this earth so that . . .

Susan, give so that . . .

Melissa, serve so that . . .

Nancy, obey so that . . .

Karla, teach so that . . .

Donna, let your light shine so that . . .

Michele, love the unloveable so that . . .

Jill, humble yourself so that . . .

⟩⟩MY FINAL CALL TO ACTION:

After spending the last five chapters with God and the call to *Living So That*, what is your final call to action? Choose one giant step of obedience you want to take for God that will allow your light to shine.

LET'S CLOSE OUR TIME TOGETHER IN PRAYER:

Heavenly Father, as we turn this last page, I want to thank You for each precious woman who has journeyed through this study with me. Thank You that You have found her faithful. May she sense Your pleasure with her hard work and commitment. Give her perfect recall of the words she has hidden in her heart. Help her to continue to apply all that she has learned. Empower her to live out her calls to action. And compel her to continue on in her study of the Word. When she begins her next journey with You, guide her down Your paths, lead her through Your Truth, and teach her Your ways. Draw her close and take her deeper still with You. I ask this in Jesus' name. Amen.

❧ Notes ❧

CHAPTER 1: JESUS CAME SO THAT . . .

1. David Jeremiah, *The Book of Romans*, vol. 2, *Man's Ruin and Christ's Redemption* (San Diego: Turning Point for God, 2000), 105.
2. Kenneth S. Wuest, *Romans in the Greek New Testament* (Grand Rapids: Wm. B. Eerdmans, 1955), 96–97.
3. John Calvin, *Institutes of the Christian Religion* (Louisville: Westminster John Knox, 2001), 82.
4. J. Vernon McGee, *The Gospels, John Chapters 11–21*, Thru the Bible Commentary Series (Nashville: Thomas Nelson, 1991), 119.

CHAPTER 2: GOD SPOKE SO THAT . . .

1. Thomas Bevers, "The Preciousness of the Bible," Sermons.Logos.com, October 2008, http://sermons.logos.com/submissions/69777-The-Preciousness-of-the-Bible#content=/submissions/69777; W. J. Federer, *Great Quotations: A Collection of Passages, Phrases and Quotations* (St. Louis: Amerisearch, 2001).
2. James Strong, *The New Strong's Expanded Exhaustive Concordance of the Bible*, Red Letter ed. (Nashville: Thomas Nelson, 2010), 739. Note that, unless otherwise indicated, the definitions of most or all Hebrew and Greek words in this book are from this source.
3. David Jeremiah, *Romans*, the Living by Faith series, vol. 6, *Romans 15–16: Staying Together and Reaching Out* (San Diego: Turning Point for God, 2003), 118.
4. Gavin Childress, *Opening Up Luke's Gospel*, Opening Up Commentary (Leominster: Day One Publications), 2006, 8–10.
5. T. R. McNeal, *Holman Illustrated Bible Dictionary* (Nashville: Holman Bible Publishers, 2003), 1057.
7. Bill Elliff, "When I Kept Silent," *Spirit of Revival* magazine, Life Action Ministries, September 1995, 20.
8. Bevers, "The Preciousness of the Bible."

CHAPTER 3: PRAY SO THAT . . .

1. Sylvia Gunter, *Prayer Portions* (Birmingham: The Father's Business, 1991), 10.
2. Marilynn Chadwick, *Sometimes He Whispers, Sometimes He Roars: Learning to Hear the Voice of God* (New York: Howard, 2012), 28.

3. Rick Warren, *The Purpose Driven Life: What on Earth Am I Here For?* exp. ed. (Grand Rapids: Zondervan, 2012), 114.

4. Carole Lewis, *A Thankful Heart: How Gratitude Brings Hope and Healing to Our Lives* (Ventura, CA: Regal, 2005), 43.

5. Matthew Henry, *Matthew Henry's Commentary of the Whole Bible* (Peabody, MA: Hendrickson Publishers, 1994), 1756–1757.

6. Rick Warren, "Rick Warren/*Purpose Driven Life* Author" (text from an interview), accessed August 5, 2013, http://www.donotgiveup.net/PurposeDrivenAuthorArticle.htm.

7. Gunter, *Prayer Portions*, 10.

8. David Jeremiah, *The Blessings and Behavior of the Believer,* Book of Ephesians, vol. 1 (San Diego: Turning Point for God, 2004), 10.

9. L. O. Richards, *The Bible Reader's Companion* (Wheaton, IL: Victor Books, 1991), electronic edition, 641.

CHAPTER 4: TRIALS COME SO THAT . . .

1. Wendy Blight, *Hidden Joy in a Dark Corner: The Transforming Power of God's Story* (Chicago: Moody, 2009), 11.

2. Warren W. Wiersbe, *The Bible Exposition Commentary, James* (Wheaton, IL: Victor Books, 1996).

3. Warren W. Wiersbe, *The Bible Exposition Commentary, 2 Corinthians* (Wheaton, IL: Victor Books, 1996).

4. Ibid.

5. Ibid.

6. David Jeremiah, *Romans*, the Living by Faith series, vol. 3: *The Sons of God and the Spirit of God* (San Diego: Turning Point for God, 2000).

7. L. O. Richards, *The Teacher's Commentary* (Wheaton, IL: Victor Books, 1987), 730.

8. Renee Swope, *A Confident Heart: How to Stop Doubting Yourself & Live in the Security of God's Promises* (Grand Rapids: Baker, 2011), 113.

9. George Mueller as quoted on The Salvation Army's Prayer Fellowship: August 2005; accessed September 3, 2013, http://www1.salvationarmy.org/prayer.nsf/9c1bbf1e422b692d86256b3c0076222d/.eb8c6bedfe756d3486257030004cda5e!OpenDocument.

10. Arthur Tappan Pierson, *George Müller of Bristol*, Appendix N, "The Wise Sayings of George Müller" (London: J. Nisbet, 1899), 439.

11. William Barclay, *The Letters to the Corinthians (The New Daily Study Bible)* (Louisville: Westminster John Knox Press, 2002), 202.

12. Richard J. Foster and James Bryan Smith, eds., *Devotional Classics: Selected Readings for Individuals and Groups* (New York: HarperSanFrancisco, 1993), 36. This devotional contains excerpts from John's *The Dark Night of the Soul*.

CHAPTER 5: LET YOUR LIGHT SHINE SO THAT . . .

1. Marcus T. C. Gould, *A collection of many select and Christian epistles, letters and testimonies, written on sundry occasions, by that ancient, eminent, faithful Friend and minister of Christ Jesus, George Fox*, Google eBook (1831), 90.
2. John Piper, *A Godward Life: Savoring the Supremacy of God in All of Life* (Sisters, OR: Multnomah, 1999), 322.
3. Beth Moore, *The Beloved Disciple: Following John to the Heart of Jesus* (Nashville: Broadman & Holman, 2003), 206.
4. Nancy Leigh DeMoss, *Choosing Forgiveness: Your Journey to Freedom* (Chicago: Moody, 2006), 29.
5. Beth Moore, *Breaking Free: Making Liberty in Christ a Reality in Life* (Nashville: Lifeway, 1999), 104.
6. Wendy Blight, *Hidden Joy in a Dark Corner: The Transforming Power of God's Story* (Chicago: Moody, 2009), 89.
7. Richard J. Foster and James Bryan Smith, eds., *Devotional Classics: Selected Readings for Individuals and Groups* (New York: HarperSanFrancisco, 1993), 272.

Proverbs 31
MINISTRIES

About Proverbs 31 Ministries

If you were inspired by *Living So That* and desire to deepen your own personal relationship with Jesus Christ, I encourage you to connect with Proverbs 31 Ministries.

Proverbs 31 Ministries exists to be a trusted friend who will take you by the hand and walk by your side, leading you one step closer to the heart of God through:

- free online daily devotions
- COMPEL writing community
- daily radio program
- books and resources
- online Bible studies

To learn more about Proverbs 31 Ministries, call 877-731-4663 or visit www.Proverbs31.org.

Proverbs 31 Ministries
630 Team Rd., Suite 100
Matthews, NC 28105
www.Proverbs31.org

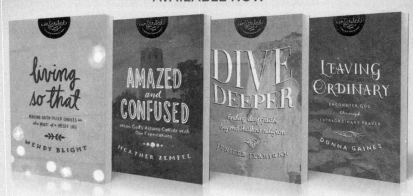